Goliath's Reckoning: Unveiling the Biassed Truth Behind Children's Court that discriminates against Fathers

How the Best Interests of the Child Can Topple State-Sanctioned Race and Gender Discrimination

Baza kuSazi

By Salatiso

Copyright

Dedication

To my father,
for and with my son,
my nephews, uncles & cousins,
brothers and friends,
boys & men,
All the fathers that have inspired me.
NK, I am so grateful for the support, thank you.

iSazisi

"During my lifetime, I have dedicated myself to this struggle of the African people.
I have fought against white domination, and I have fought against black domination.
I have cherished the ideal of a democratic and free society in which all persons live together in harmony and with equal opportunities.
It is an ideal which I hope to live for and to achieve. But if needs be, it is an ideal for which I am prepared to die."
Nelson Mandela

Introduction: The Power Within

In an era where personal agency often seems diminished by the dictates of experts and institutional systems, it is all too easy to feel powerless, especially when confronting the structures that govern our lives. My journey, as a father fighting for the rights of my son and challenging a biassed legal system, has laid bare the stark realities of this power imbalance. Yet, it has also illuminated the profound strength that resides within each of us when we stand up for what is right.

This book is born from a deeply personal struggle, a battle waged not only for my son but for my nephews, Solo and all other boys and men who will one day stand where I stand now. It is a testament to the enduring power of the principle that all are equal before the law, a principle that empowers even the smallest voice to challenge the mightiest adversaries. In a society where state-sanctioned discrimination, whether by race or gender, is justified in the name of redress, this principle becomes a beacon of hope and justice.

Growing up, the stories of my parents, instilled in me the values of resilience and steadfastness. As a Xhosa man, my spiritual connection to traditional beliefs sometimes conflicted with the Christian principles around me, yet this duality offered me profound insights. Among these insights is a deep reverence for universal truths found in various texts, including the Bible.

The biblical tale of David and Goliath resonates strongly with me as I challenge the systemic biases in South Africa's family courts—a system that often favours mothers and marginalises fathers, to the detriment of children's best interests. Like David, who faced a formidable opponent with only his faith and a sling, I confront a powerful legal system, armed with love for my son and nephews, and the unwavering belief in a just cause.

This book is not only about my personal journey. It is a tool for fighting against all forms of state-sanctioned discrimination, highlighting how policies intended for redress have, ironically, perpetuated new forms of inequality. In South Africa, where the pursuit of historical redress has too often led to policies that undermine the future, our children—the "born free" generation—now grapple with poverty, high unemployment, and other social ills. The very policies designed to right historical wrongs have, in practice, compromised the best interests of the child and the broader society.

As you read through these pages, you will find a blend of personal narrative and practical strategies, designed to empower other parents—especially fathers—who find themselves battling a system that seems rigged against them. This book aims to inspire a movement towards genuine equality before the law, where every child benefits from the love, guidance, and support of both parents, and by extension, the whole family, including grandparents.

The essence of this book is to reaffirm the principle that no one, regardless of their social standing or background, should feel small or powerless. Equality before the law is not merely a legal ideal but a living principle that ensures everyone has the ability to hold the state and its institutions accountable. It is a principle that must prevail, not just for fathers, but for the benefit of the entire family and, above all, in the best interests of the child.

Drawing strength from the examples of those who have gone before us—from mythical heroes like David to the everyday champions in our own lives—I invite you to recognize and harness the power within yourself. Together, we can create a world where justice and true equality reign, a world where every child, regardless of race or gender, can grow up in a society that cherishes their rights and nurtures their potential.

Welcome to the journey.

Part I: Critique of Formal Systems

1. The Erosion of Personal Autonomy and the Rise of Formal Systems

In democratic societies, individual freedom and personal autonomy are often touted as core values. However, upon closer examination, it becomes evident that even in these systems, there are significant constraints on true individual choice. One of the most glaring examples of this paradox is the practice of compulsory taxation.

Citizens are compelled, under the threat of legal consequences, to surrender a portion of their income to the government. This form of extortion is justified as necessary for the functioning of society, but it also exposes the illusion of freedom in democratic systems.

Ironically, the funds collected through taxation are often used to establish and sustain institutions that further erode personal autonomy, such as public schools, healthcare systems, and legal frameworks that dictate personal choices.

1.1. The Origins of Formal Systems and the Erosion of Personal Autonomy

The erosion of personal autonomy can be traced back to the emergence of formal systems and the growing reliance on credentialed experts. As societies became more complex and specialised throughout history, there was a gradual shift towards institutionalised knowledge and decision-making.

The development of formal education systems, professional associations, and regulatory bodies led to the rise of an "expert class" that began to wield significant influence over personal choices. As these formal systems gained power and legitimacy, individuals increasingly deferred to the opinions and recommendations of credentialed experts, often at the expense of their own intuition, experiences, and contextual knowledge.

While formal systems initially aimed to provide structure and standardisation, their peak often marked the beginning of their destructive consequences, as they began to erode personal autonomy and stifle individuality and choice.

1.2. The Erosion of Parental Rights in Child-Rearing

One of the most striking examples of the erosion of personal autonomy is the increasing role of formal schools and credentialed experts in child-rearing decisions. In many societies, parents are compelled, either through legal mandates or strong social pressure, to enrol their children in formal education systems.

This mandatory schooling separates children from the direct care and education of their parents, placing them under the influence of teachers and administrators who may not share the same values, beliefs, or cultural background. The curriculum and teaching methods are often determined by educational authorities and credentialed experts, leaving little room for parental input or customization based on individual needs and preferences.

This erosion of parental rights in child-rearing devalues the knowledge and experience of parents, who are often best equipped to make decisions about their children's development and well-being.

1.3. The Illusion of Expertise

The rise of the "expert class" has led to a widespread belief in the superiority of credentialed expertise over individual knowledge and experience. However, this belief is often an illusion, as expertise in one narrow field does not necessarily translate to wisdom in all areas of life.

The limitations of credentialed expertise become apparent when considering the complexities of personal decision-making, which often involve a wide range of factors, including individual values, cultural background, and unique life experiences. While experts can provide valuable information and insights, their recommendations should not be blindly followed without critical evaluation and personal reflection.

The illusion of expertise can lead to a dangerous erosion of personal autonomy, as individuals increasingly defer to the opinions of credentialed experts rather than trusting their own judgement and intuition.

1.4. The Devaluation of Personal Opinions and Experiences

As formal systems and credentialed experts gain prominence, there is often a corresponding devaluation of personal opinions and experiences. Society begins to place greater value on conformity to mainstream ideas and practices, rather than encouraging diverse perspectives and individual expression.

Dissenting voices and alternative viewpoints are often marginalised or dismissed as uninformed or misguided, creating a climate of groupthink and intellectual homogeneity. This devaluation of personal opinions and experiences can have a chilling effect on critical thinking and individual autonomy, as people become less willing to express their unique perspectives and challenge prevailing norms.

The pressure to conform to mainstream opinions and practices can lead to a loss of creativity, innovation, and personal growth, as individuals suppress their authentic selves in favour of fitting in with the crowd.

1.5. The Role of External Experts in Dictating Personal Choices

The erosion of personal autonomy is further exacerbated by the increasing reliance on external experts in making personal choices, particularly in the realms of health and education. From medical treatment decisions to educational pathways, individuals are often pressured to defer to the recommendations of credentialed professionals, even when these recommendations may not align with their personal values, preferences, or instincts.

This outsourcing of personal decision-making to external experts can lead to a loss of agency and self-determination, as individuals become passive recipients of expert advice rather than active participants in shaping their own lives. The potential consequences of this erosion of personal autonomy are significant, as individuals may make choices that are not truly their own, leading to feelings of disempowerment, resentment, and a lack of fulfilment.

1.6. Vaccine Mandates during COVID-19: A Case Study in the Erosion of Personal Autonomy

The COVID-19 pandemic has brought the debate surrounding personal autonomy and the role of credentialed experts into sharp focus, particularly in the context of vaccine mandates. As governments and public health authorities have pushed for widespread vaccination, there has been a heated debate about the balance between individual choice and public health concerns.

Proponents of vaccine mandates argue that they are necessary to protect public health and prevent the spread of the virus, while opponents view them as a violation of personal autonomy and informed consent. The rise of vaccine mandates has highlighted the power of credentialed experts and public institutions in shaping personal medical decisions, often overriding individual preferences and concerns.

This case study illustrates the ongoing tension between personal autonomy and the perceived authority of formal systems and experts in times of crisis.

1.7. The Human Existence as a Year: A Metaphor for the Rise and Fall of Formal Systems

To better understand the trajectory of formal systems and their impact on personal autonomy, it can be helpful to use the metaphor of human existence as a year. In the early stages of life, formal systems are like the spring, full of promise and potential. They emerge as a means of organising and standardising knowledge and practices, with the goal of improving efficiency and outcomes.

As formal systems develop and mature, they reach their peak, like the summer, where they are seen as the dominant and most effective means of decision-making and problem-solving. However, as formal systems become more rigid and bureaucratic, they begin to show signs of decay and dysfunction, like the autumn.

The destructive consequences of formal systems become more apparent, as they stifle innovation, creativity, and personal autonomy. In the winter of their existence, formal systems can become oppressive and harmful, leading to a loss of trust and a desire for change.

1.8. Reclaiming Personal Autonomy in an Era of Formal Systems

In an era characterised by the dominance of formal systems and credentialed experts, it is more important than ever to reclaim personal autonomy and embrace individual responsibility in decision-making. While experts and formal systems can provide valuable information and guidance, they should not be the sole determinants of personal choices.

Individuals must cultivate the critical thinking skills and self-awareness necessary to navigate the complexities of modern life, drawing on a balance of expert knowledge and personal experiences. Education and empowerment are key to promoting personal autonomy and informed choice, as they equip individuals with the tools and confidence to make decisions that align with their values and goals.

By reclaiming personal autonomy and resisting the erosion of individual choice, we can create a society that values diversity, creativity, and the unique contributions of every individual.

2. Parenting in the African Context: The Xhosa Perspective

Parenting in the African context, particularly among the Xhosa people, is deeply rooted in cultural traditions, values, and beliefs. The role of a parent extends beyond providing for the physical needs of a child, encompassing the imparting of cultural knowledge, values, and a sense of identity. The Xhosa culture emphasises community, spirituality, and the interconnectedness of family members, shaping a unique approach to child-rearing that is both nurturing and holistic. The age-old traditions and practices passed down through generations have played a pivotal role in shaping the values and identity of the Xhosa people, instilling a sense of pride, resilience, and unity within the community.

It is important to acknowledge the value of traditional knowledge and practices, even in the face of modern scientific advancements. While science has undoubtedly contributed to our understanding of the world and has led to remarkable discoveries, it is not the only source of wisdom and guidance. The origins of the universe, for example, remain a mystery that science has yet to fully unravel. Until we can definitively explain the singularity that preceded the Big Bang, it is prudent to maintain a healthy respect for the traditional, informal, and often unarticulated knowledge that has sustained our ancestors for generations.

My own mother, who has been an instrumental figure in shaping the man I am today, possesses no formal qualifications in parenting. This is true for the vast majority of parents throughout history. The absence of a formal education in child-rearing does not diminish the value of the wisdom and experience passed down through generations. The fact that traditional parenting practices are not always documented or articulated in academic terms does not negate their effectiveness or significance.

Long before the advent of the scientific method, writing, and the formalisation of knowledge, our ancestors relied on tradition to guide them in raising their children. These traditions, honed over centuries of trial and error, have proven to be resilient and adaptable, ensuring the survival and flourishing of communities in the face of countless challenges.

As we explore the Xhosa perspective on parenting, which is not that different from most traditional systems, within Africa and beyond, it is crucial to approach the topic with an open mind and a deep respect for the cultural heritage that has shaped these practices. By understanding and appreciating the traditional wisdom of our ancestors, we can gain valuable insights into the art of child-rearing and the importance of preserving our cultural identity in an ever-changing world.

In the following sections, we will delve deeper into the specific aspects of Xhosa parenting, examining the roles of family and community, the impact of spirituality, and the ways in which these traditions continue to influence contemporary parenting practices. Through this exploration, we aim to highlight the enduring value of traditional knowledge and the lessons we can learn from the Xhosa approach to nurturing and guiding the next generation.

2.1. The Role of Family and Extended Family as a Support Base

In many cultures, including the Xhosa, the family and extended family play a crucial role in child-rearing. Grandparents, aunts, uncles, and other relatives actively participate in the upbringing of children, offering emotional support, guidance, and wisdom. This collective approach to parenting creates a robust support network that fosters a sense of belonging, security, and cultural identity. The bond between family members is strengthened through shared experiences, traditions, and values, contributing to the overall well-being and development of children within the community.

2.2. The Threat of Properly Functioning Families to Governments and Systems Seeking to Undermine Personal Autonomy

Properly functioning families pose a threat to the authority of governments and formal systems that seek to undermine parental rights and autonomy. Strong family units encourage independent thinking, cultural preservation, and a reduced reliance on external institutions and experts.

The erosion of parental rights and autonomy not only undermines the well-being of children but also threatens the cultural integrity and resilience of communities, leading to a loss of cultural identity and connection to ancestral roots.

2.3. The Rise of Experts and Surrogates: Historical Context

The rise of experts and surrogates in child-rearing can be traced back to the industrial revolution and the subsequent shift towards urbanisation and modernization. As societies became more complex and specialised, there was a growing emphasis on formal education, professional expertise, and institutionalised systems of care.

This shift gradually eroded the traditional roles and authority of parents, placing increasing reliance on credentialed experts and formal systems. The marginalisation of indigenous knowledge and practices, coupled with the commodification of childcare, has led to the proliferation of "experts" and surrogates who often prioritise profit over the well-being and cultural preservation of children.

2.4. The Snake Oil Salesman: Exploiting Parental Fears for Profit

In the modern era, the "snake oil salesman" represents the unscrupulous individuals and organisations that exploit parental fears and insecurities for financial gain. Through targeted marketing, misleading information, and false promises, these entities undermine parental confidence and encourage a greater reliance on "expert" advice and solutions. The proliferation of these misleading and harmful practices further erodes parental rights and autonomy, leading to a loss of trust in traditional and community-based child-rearing practices.

2.5. The Increasing Reliance on Experts and Formal Systems in South Africa: Historical and Socio-Economic Factors

In South Africa, the increasing reliance on experts and formal systems in child-rearing has been influenced by various factors, including historical, socio-economic, and political dynamics. The legacy of apartheid, socio-economic disparities, and the perceived authority of Western educational and medical systems have contributed to the erosion of parental rights and the marginalisation of indigenous knowledge and practices. The implementation of policies and regulations that prioritise formal education, professional expertise, and institutionalised care over traditional and community-based child-rearing practices has further exacerbated the problem, leading to a loss of cultural identity, autonomy, and resilience within communities.

2.6. The Importance of Parental Guidance Despite Lack of Official Certification

Despite the lack of official parenting certification, the importance of parental guidance, love, and nurturing cannot be overstated. Parents possess a unique understanding of their children's needs, personalities, and cultural background, enabling them to provide personalised care and guidance that formal systems and experts often overlook or misunderstand.

The bond between parent and child is strengthened through shared experiences, trust, and unconditional love, creating a nurturing and supportive environment that fosters emotional, cognitive, and cultural development. It is crucial to recognize and value the wisdom and expertise of parents, empowering them to reclaim their rightful role as the primary caregivers and educators of their children.

2.7. Reclaiming Parental Rights and Autonomy

The erosion of parental rights and autonomy is a pressing issue that requires urgent attention and advocacy. By understanding the historical context, cultural values, and societal influences that have contributed to this trend, we can work towards reclaiming parental rights, empowering families, and fostering a more equitable and just society. In the following chapters, we will explore practical strategies, tools, and insights to empower parents, challenge the prevailing narrative, and advocate for the importance of parental guidance in child-rearing.

3. The Double-Edged Sword of Digitalization

The digital age has fundamentally transformed our world, reshaping how we communicate, learn, work, and engage with society. On one hand, the internet and digital tools have democratised access to information, connected us across borders, and opened up new avenues for self-expression and entrepreneurship.

Yet, this same landscape is rife with threats to personal autonomy, from pervasive data surveillance to the monopolisation of information by a handful of tech giants. As we navigate this digital frontier, we must learn to harness its potential for empowerment while building resilience against its pitfalls. This chapter will explore strategies for asserting autonomy in the face of digital challenges, leveraging technology as a tool for personal growth and collective action.

3.1. Navigating Digital Surveillance

3.1.1. **Understanding the Landscape:** In our digitally interconnected world, our every online action leaves a trace. Corporations collect vast troves of personal data, tracking our browsing habits, purchases, and social interactions to profile us for targeted advertising. Governments engage in mass surveillance programs in the name of national security. Our smartphones beacon our locations, our smart homes listen in on our conversations. This pervasive surveillance threatens the very core of privacy and autonomy. To protect ourselves, we must first understand the scope of this monitoring and the entities behind it.

3.1.2. **Protecting Your Digital Self:** While complete anonymity online is nearly impossible, we can take steps to minimise our digital footprints and protect sensitive information. Encryption is a key tool, scrambling our data so that intercepted communications are indecipherable to surveillance systems. Virtual Private Networks (VPNs) can mask our online activities by routing internet traffic through secure servers. Secure messaging apps like Signal employ end-to-end encryption to prevent interception. Beyond technical solutions, practising 'digital hygiene' - being cautious about what information we share online, using strong and unique passwords, and regularly auditing our privacy settings - is critical. By proactively safeguarding our digital selves, we maintain a degree of autonomy in the face of surveillance.

3.2. The Monopolization of Information

3.2.1. **Tech Giants and Information Control**: A handful of tech companies - Google, Facebook, Amazon, Apple - have an outsized influence over the information we consume. Their algorithms curate our news feeds, search results, and product recommendations, often prioritising engagement over truth. This concentration of power allows for the manipulation of public opinion, the spread of misinformation, and the stifling of dissenting voices. When our information diets are controlled by a few corporate entities, our capacity for independent thought and choice is diminished. Recognizing this threat is the first step in resisting it.

3.2.2. **Seeking Alternative Voices:** To counteract the homogenising force of Big Tech, we must actively seek out diverse perspectives and support decentralised information ecosystems. This means looking beyond mainstream social media and news aggregators to independent journalism, community-driven forums, and open-source knowledge bases. It means supporting initiatives that prioritise privacy, transparency, and user control over data. Diversifying our information sources and digital communities empowers us to break free from corporate narratives and engage with a plurality of ideas, a cornerstone of autonomous thinking.

3.3. Harnessing Digital Tools for Empowerment

3.3.1. Educational Resources: The internet is a goldmine of educational opportunities, many available free of cost, a topic a covered on The Homeschooling Father. Massive Open Online Courses (MOOCs) from top universities allow anyone with an internet connection to learn from world-class instructors. Skill-sharing platforms like Skillshare and YouTube tutorials enable us to gain practical skills on demand. Open access journals and digital libraries put a wealth of academic knowledge at our fingertips. By taking advantage of these resources, we can pursue self-directed learning, expand our knowledge base, and develop new competencies, all essential for personal growth and autonomy in a rapidly evolving world.

3.3.2. Building Online Communities: One of the greatest strengths of the internet is its ability to connect people across geographic and social boundaries. Online communities, whether organised around shared interests, identities, or goals, offer spaces for mutual support, collaboration, and collective action. From forums for niche hobbies to global activist networks, these digital spaces allow individuals to find their tribes, share knowledge, and amplify their voices. By actively participating in and contributing to online communities, we can forge meaningful connections, build solidarity, and work together towards common aims. This collective empowerment is a potent force for asserting autonomy in the face of systemic challenges.

3.4. Digital Entrepreneurship and Autonomy

3.4.1. The New Economy: The digital landscape has given rise to new economic models that prioritise autonomy, flexibility, and purpose. Online marketplaces like Etsy and Fiverr allow individuals to monetize their crafts and skills directly. Platforms like Patreon and Substack enable creators to build subscription-based income streams from their artistic and intellectual work. The gig economy, for all its faults, offers opportunities for freelancers to work on their own terms. These digital economic pathways, while not without challenges, provide alternatives to traditional employment structures and empower individuals to pursue livelihoods aligned with their values and desires.

3.4.2. Strategies for Success: To thrive as a digital entrepreneur, one must be strategic in leveraging online tools and platforms. Building a strong personal brand is essential, as is identifying and catering to a specific niche or audience. Developing a robust online presence across multiple channels - a website, social media profiles, content platforms - increases visibility and reach. Collaborating with other creators and participating in online communities can lead to valuable partnerships and support networks. Continuously updating one's skills and adapting to new technologies is also critical in a fast-paced digital economy. By approaching digital entrepreneurship with intention and resilience, individuals can carve out autonomous paths in an increasingly interconnected world.

3.5. Ethical Considerations in the Digital Realm

3.5.1. Navigating Ethical Dilemmas: As we engage with digital tools and spaces, we are confronted with a range of ethical dilemmas. How do we balance the benefits of personalization with the risks of data mining? What responsibility do we bear for the content we share and the information we consume? How do we navigate tensions between free speech and harmful misinformation? Grappling with these questions requires digital literacy - not just technical skills, but critical thinking about the implications of our online actions.

It demands that we approach our digital lives with intentionality, considering the impact of our choices on ourselves, our communities, and society at large.

3.5.2. Promoting a Fair Digital Future: Ultimately, building autonomy in the digital age is not just a personal endeavour, but a collective one. The policies and norms that govern digital spaces are shaped by the actions and advocacy of citizens, technologists, and policymakers. By participating in digital governance debates, supporting initiatives for digital equity and inclusion, and demanding accountability from tech companies and governments, we can work towards a future where digital tools serve the interests of individual autonomy and social good. This requires ongoing engagement, learning, and activism from all of us as digital citizens.

3.6. Conclusion: The Autonomous Digital Citizen

As we navigate the uncharted territories of the digital age, let us envision a path towards becoming autonomous digital citizens. This means using digital tools with purpose and discernment, cultivating resilience against their potential harms, and harnessing their power for personal growth and social change. It means approaching our online lives with the same intentionality and integrity we bring to our offline interactions. It means contributing to digital communities and economies in ways that align with our values and support collective flourishing.

The challenges of the digital age are formidable, but so too are the opportunities. By asserting our autonomy in digital spaces, we not only reclaim our own agency, but shape a future where technology empowers rather than constraints human potential. The autonomous digital citizen is not a final destination, but an ongoing journey of adaptability, critical engagement, and purposeful action in an ever-evolving landscape. As we embark on this path, let us do so with courage, wisdom, and a steadfast commitment to our individual and collective freedoms.

Part II: Challenging the Status Quo

4. The Shortcomings of Formal Systems in South Africa

As South Africa grapples with the challenges of the post-apartheid era, the failures of formal systems have become increasingly apparent. From education to healthcare, electricity to municipal services, the reliance on credentials and the dismissal of informal systems have led to a crisis of competence and integrity. Drawing on the principles outlined in "The Homeschooling Father, Why and How I Got Started," this chapter will explore the shortcomings of formal systems in South Africa and the potential for alternative approaches, such as homeschooling, to address these issues.

4.1. The Education Crisis

The education system in South Africa has long been a topic of concern, with numerous challenges hindering its ability to provide quality education to all students. Despite efforts to reform and improve the system, many issues persist, leading to a suboptimal learning environment for the nation's youth.

In this section, we will delve into the specific problems plaguing the formal education system, including overcrowding, underfunding, and a lack of qualified teachers. We will also explore how the one-size-fits-all approach, as mentioned in "The Homeschooling Father," fails to cater to the diverse needs of students.

Furthermore, we will examine how the emphasis on credentials over competence and the neglect of indigenous knowledge systems have contributed to the deterioration of educational quality in South Africa.

4.2. The Formal Education System's Challenges

4.2.1. **Overcrowding:** Many schools in South Africa, particularly in urban areas, are severely overcrowded. Classrooms designed for 30-40 students often accommodate 50 or more, leading to a compromised learning environment. This overcrowding makes it difficult for teachers to provide individual attention to students, hindering their ability to address specific learning needs and ensure that all students are keeping up with the curriculum.

4.2.2. **Underfunding:** The education system in South Africa is chronically underfunded, with many schools lacking basic resources such as textbooks, computers, and laboratory equipment. This lack of funding also results in poorly maintained infrastructure, with some schools lacking proper sanitation facilities or even running water. The financial constraints make it challenging for schools to attract and retain qualified teachers, further exacerbating the quality of education provided.

4.2.3. **Lack of Qualified Teachers:** The shortage of qualified teachers is a significant problem in South Africa's education system. Many teachers lack the necessary subject knowledge and pedagogical skills to effectively teach their students. This issue is particularly prevalent in rural areas, where it is difficult to attract and retain qualified educators. The lack of qualified teachers leads to a lower quality of instruction and, consequently, poorer educational outcomes for students.

4.3. The Pitfalls of a One-Size-Fits-All Approach

4.3.1. **Diverse Learning Needs:** As highlighted in "The Homeschooling Father," the traditional schooling system often adopts a one-size-fits-all approach that fails to accommodate the diverse learning needs and styles of individual students. Children have different strengths, weaknesses, and interests, and a uniform curriculum may not effectively cater to these differences. This rigid approach can lead to some students struggling to keep up, while others may feel unchallenged and disengaged.

4.3.2. **Lack of Flexibility:** The formal education system often lacks the flexibility to adapt to the unique circumstances and backgrounds of students. For example, students from disadvantaged communities may face additional challenges, such as poverty, malnutrition, and limited access to educational resources. A one-size-fits-all approach may not adequately address these challenges, leading to a widening achievement gap between advantaged and disadvantaged students.

4.4. The Emphasis on Credentials Over Competence

4.4.1. **Proliferation of Unqualified Educators:** The emphasis on credentials over competence has led to a situation where many educators and administrators in the formal education system lack the necessary skills and knowledge to effectively perform their roles. Some individuals may have obtained their positions through nepotism, political connections, or even fraudulent qualifications. This proliferation of unqualified educators compromises the quality of education provided to students.

4.4.2. **Neglect of Practical Skills:** The focus on credentials often comes at the expense of practical skills and real-world experience. The formal education system tends to prioritise theoretical knowledge and academic achievements over the development of practical skills that are valuable in the workforce and everyday life. This neglect of practical skills can leave students ill-prepared for the challenges they will face after completing their formal education.

4.5. The Neglect of Indigenous Knowledge Systems

4.5.1. **Cultural Disconnect:** The formal education system in South Africa has largely been modelled after Western education systems, often neglecting the rich indigenous knowledge systems and cultural heritage of the nation. This neglect can lead to a cultural disconnect for many students, who may feel that their own cultural backgrounds and experiences are not valued or represented in the curriculum.

4.5.2. **Loss of Practical Skills:** Indigenous knowledge systems often place a strong emphasis on practical skills and the application of knowledge in real-world contexts. The neglect of these knowledge systems in the formal education system can result in students missing out on valuable opportunities to develop practical skills that are relevant to their communities and daily lives. This loss of practical skills can limit students' ability to contribute to their communities and succeed in various aspects of life outside of the formal education setting.

4.5.3. Homeschooling: A Catalyst for Educational Reform and Societal Transformation

The shortcomings of South Africa's formal education system are glaringly evident in the challenges faced by the post-apartheid generation. Despite increased enrollment and investment, educational outcomes have stagnated, and social ills such as unemployment, crime, and inequality continue to plague the nation. This crisis necessitates a fundamental re-evaluation of the role of education and a bold exploration of alternative models that prioritize the holistic development of children, empower parents, and value diverse knowledge systems.

Homeschooling, as discussed in "The Homeschooling Father," emerges as a promising alternative that can address many of the systemic issues plaguing the formal education system. By embracing personalised learning, parental involvement, and the integration of practical skills and cultural knowledge, homeschooling can empower children to reach their full potential and contribute to a more equitable and prosperous society.

The traditional one-size-fits-all approach of formal schooling often fails to cater to the diverse learning styles and needs of individual students. In contrast, homeschooling allows parents to tailor education to their child's unique strengths, weaknesses, and interests, fostering a love of learning and a sense of ownership over their educational journey. This personalised approach can lead to improved academic performance, increased engagement, and a deeper understanding of the subject matter.

Furthermore, homeschooling empowers parents to take an active role in their children's education, fostering a stronger parent-child bond and a more supportive learning environment. By actively participating in their child's learning journey, parents can provide guidance, encouragement, and mentorship, instilling values and life skills that are often overlooked in the formal school setting.

In addition to academic and personal development, homeschooling also allows for the integration of practical skills and cultural knowledge that are often neglected in the traditional curriculum. By incorporating real-world experiences, hands-on learning, and cultural traditions, homeschooling can equip children with the skills and knowledge necessary to thrive in a rapidly changing world.

The benefits of homeschooling extend beyond individual children and families. By reducing the burden on the formal education system, homeschooling can free up resources to improve the quality of education for those who remain in traditional schools. Additionally, by fostering a generation of critical thinkers, innovators, and problem solvers, homeschooling can contribute to the development of a more dynamic and resilient society.

The adoption of homeschooling as a viable alternative to formal schooling can serve as a catalyst for broader educational reform. By demonstrating the effectiveness of personalised learning, parental involvement, and the integration of diverse knowledge systems, homeschooling can inspire changes in the traditional education system, leading to a more inclusive, equitable, and effective approach to education.

In conclusion, the challenges faced by South Africa's post-apartheid generation highlight the urgent need for educational reform. Homeschooling offers a promising alternative that can empower children, parents, and communities to create a brighter future for the country. By embracing this flexible and personalised approach to education, we can unlock the full potential of our children and build a more equitable and prosperous society for all.

5. Beyond Parchment: The Broken Promises of the Rainbow Nation

Thirty years after apartheid's end, South Africa's promise of a better life for all remains unfulfilled. Crumbling infrastructure, persistent water shortages, and rolling blackouts paint a bleak picture of a nation in crisis. This systemic failure isn't due to a lack of qualified professionals; it's a consequence of governance failures, corruption, and an over-reliance on formal credentials that have masked deeper issues.

Johannesburg, the nation's economic heart, exemplifies this crisis. Despite its "world-class" aspirations, the city's water infrastructure is in shambles. Millions of residents, predominantly in impoverished townships, endure extended water outages. This neglect of basic needs is mirrored in other cities like Cape Town and Gqeberha, where Day Zero looms ominously.

The electricity grid, managed by the beleaguered Eskom, further illustrates this dysfunction. Despite its credentialed leadership, Eskom is crippled by mismanagement and corruption, leading to frequent blackouts that disproportionately harm poor communities.

Waste management, too, has collapsed. Uncollected garbage piles up, posing health risks and environmental hazards, especially in densely populated townships. This breakdown of essential services reflects a wider pattern of governance failures at all levels.

While affirmative action was intended to redress historical injustices, its implementation has sometimes prioritised demographics over merit, further eroding service delivery. This, coupled with rampant corruption and a lack of accountability, has created a vicious cycle of mismanagement and neglect. South Africa's crisis is a stark reminder that formal qualifications alone cannot guarantee competence or ethical leadership. As the nation reflects on three decades of democracy, it's time to re-evaluate the overreliance on credentials and embrace a more holistic approach to governance that prioritises practical skills, accountability, and the needs of all citizens.

5.1. The Illusion of Public Health: A Crumbling Foundation in South Africa

The South African public health system, like the education system, presents an illusion of functionality. Staffed with credentialed professionals and supported by significant government expenditure, it promises quality care to all citizens. However, beneath the surface, the system is crumbling, plagued by systemic failures that have devastating consequences for individuals and communities.

The financial burden of medical malpractice claims on the Gauteng Department of Health is staggering. In the 2020/2021 financial year alone, over R500 million was paid out in claims, with an additional R2.4 billion in contingent liabilities for ongoing cases. These figures reveal a disturbing trend of negligence and substandard care within the public health system, despite the presence of qualified professionals.

One tragic example is the case of a woman who gave birth to a child with cerebral palsy at Chris Hani Baragwanath Hospital in Johannesburg. Due to the staff's failure to monitor the baby's heart rate during labour, the child suffered irreversible brain damage. The family was awarded R23 million in damages, a cost ultimately borne by taxpayers. This case is not an isolated incident but rather indicative of a broader pattern of negligence and malpractice within the public health system.

Since 1994, medical malpractice claims have been steadily rising, reaching a staggering R104.5 billion in contingent liabilities in 2019/2020. This alarming increase underscores the systemic failures within the public health system, where patients are routinely subjected to substandard care, misdiagnosis, and even neglect. The human cost of these failures is immeasurable, with countless lives lost or irrevocably damaged due to preventable medical errors.

The Life Esidimeni tragedy, where over 144 psychiatric patients died due to neglect and mistreatment after being transferred to ill-equipped NGOs, is a chilling reminder of the consequences of a failing public health system. The deaths of Babita Deokaran and other whistleblowers who exposed corruption and mismanagement in the health sector further highlight the systemic issues that plague the system.

Reports of patient deaths due to negligence, suicides in understaffed hospitals, and the collapse of essential services in provinces like the Eastern Cape paint a bleak picture of the state of public health in South Africa. The COVID-19 pandemic further exposed the vulnerabilities of the system, with healthcare workers feeling betrayed by the government's inadequate response and the rampant corruption that diverted resources away from frontline care.

These failures are not simply a matter of individual negligence but rather a reflection of a deeper systemic crisis. Inadequate funding, corruption, mismanagement, and a lack of accountability have created an environment where patient safety and well-being are compromised. The consequences are dire, with devastating impacts on individuals, families, and communities.

The illusion of a functioning public health system is shattered by the reality of preventable deaths, suffering, and injustice. It is a stark reminder that credentials alone do not guarantee competence or compassion. As with the education system, the public health system in South Africa requires a fundamental re-evaluation and transformation to ensure that it truly serves the needs of the people and upholds the right to health for all.

5.2. The Illusion of Healthcare: Systemic Failures Extend to Private Sector

The illusion of a functional healthcare system in South Africa is not limited to the public sector. The private healthcare industry, despite its perceived superior resources and expertise, is equally plagued by systemic failures that result in devastating consequences for patients.

In 2020, the total value of reported medical malpractice claims against private healthcare providers reached a staggering R2.2 billion, with the average claim size increasing by 27% compared to the previous year. This alarming trend reveals that even those who can afford private care are not immune to medical negligence and substandard treatment.

One such incident involved a Johannesburg patient undergoing surgery at a private hospital for the removal of a cancerous tumour. Due to a surgical team's negligence, the patient's healthy kidney was mistakenly removed instead. The R6 million in damages awarded in this case underscores the severe consequences of medical errors, even in the private sector, where patients expect a higher standard of care.

The prevalence of medical malpractice in the private sector is not a recent phenomenon. In "The Homeschooling Father," I recount a personal experience where my partner suffered due to the negligence of a private healthcare practitioner. This incident, like the others mentioned, highlights the systemic issues that permeate both public and private healthcare in South Africa.

While the United States has seen a slight decline in medical malpractice claims since the early 2000s, the total costs associated with these claims remain high, with an estimated $4 billion paid out in 2018. This comparison reveals that the issue of medical negligence is not unique to South Africa, but the increasing trend in private healthcare malpractice claims here is a cause for serious concern.

The rising trend in private healthcare malpractice claims can be attributed to several factors, including inadequate regulation and oversight, a lack of transparency and accountability, and a culture of prioritising profits over patient safety. These issues, coupled with the high costs of private healthcare, create a perfect storm for medical errors and negligence to occur.

The impact of these failures is devastating, not only for the victims of medical malpractice but also for their families and society as a whole. The physical, emotional, and financial toll of medical errors can be immense, leaving individuals and families struggling to cope with the aftermath.

The illusion of a reliable and safe private healthcare system is shattered by the reality of preventable harm and suffering. It is imperative that South Africa addresses the systemic issues within both public and private healthcare to ensure that all citizens have access to quality care that prioritises patient safety and well-being.

5.3. A Prescription for Change: Rebuilding Trust in South Africa's Healthcare System

The failures of both public and private health institutions in South Africa, as evidenced by the rising number and value of medical malpractice claims, highlight the urgent need for reform in the healthcare system. Despite the presence of credentialed health professionals, the quality of care provided to patients has been inconsistent and, in many cases, negligent. The financial burden of these malpractice claims falls on taxpayers, as seen in the case of the Gauteng Health Department, which has paid out hundreds of millions of rands in claims.

While the situation in the United States shows some improvement in terms of the frequency of medical malpractice cases, the high costs associated with these claims remain a significant problem. The comparison between South Africa and the US underscores the global nature of the challenge of ensuring consistent, high-quality healthcare.

These findings align with the broader context of this book, which questions the overreliance on formal systems and credentials in various aspects of society. The failures of the healthcare system in South Africa, despite the presence of credentialed professionals, demonstrate that formal qualifications alone do not guarantee competence or the delivery of adequate care. As discussed in other chapters, the neglect of informal systems, such as traditional healing practices and community-based care, may also contribute to the shortcomings of the current healthcare system.

To address these challenges, a comprehensive reform of the healthcare system is necessary. This reform should focus on improving accountability, transparency, and the quality of care provided by both public and private healthcare institutions. Additionally, integrating traditional healing practices and community-based care into the formal healthcare system may help bridge the gap between formal and informal systems, ultimately leading to better health outcomes for all South Africans.

5.4. The Collapse of Municipal Services in South Africa

Johannesburg, South Africa's largest metropolis and self-styled "world-class African city," epitomises the severe and widespread water crisis affecting the nation. Over half of Johannesburg's 5.5 million residents, particularly in Soweto, have endured weeks without water. This predicament mirrors a broader, nationwide failure to fulfil post-apartheid promises of enhanced service delivery. Despite oversight by credentialed professionals, the city's water infrastructure remains severely neglected, plagued by broken pipes and failing pump stations, leading to extensive outages. This crisis hits the black majority hardest, especially those in underprivileged areas, forcing them into long queues for sporadic water supplies that often run out. Such conditions starkly reveal the inadequacies in infrastructure and the failure to address the essential needs of South Africa's most vulnerable populations. Johannesburg's struggles are not isolated. Cities across the country, from Cape Town to Pretoria, face similar challenges. In Nelson Mandela Bay, water restrictions have reached critical levels, with dam levels falling below 15%, pushing the city to the brink of Day Zero. Similarly, Gqeberha has suffered severe water shortages, exacerbated by prolonged drought and deteriorating infrastructure. These examples underscore a nationwide crisis of water management and service delivery.

South Africa's electricity woes, epitomised by Eskom's persistent load-shedding, reflect a profound national crisis in power provision. Frequent planned blackouts, sometimes extending up to 10 hours a day, disrupt daily life across the country. Eskom, despite its credentialed leadership, is crippled by mismanagement, corruption, and a chronic lack of maintenance. This failure is most acutely felt in poor communities, where unreliable electricity hampers small businesses, disrupts education, and undermines healthcare facilities. Nationally, the electricity crisis has deepened socio-economic disparities, with impoverished regions like Soweto and informal settlements bearing the brunt. In areas like the Eastern Cape and parts of Limpopo, frequent outages have become a grim norm, exacerbating existing inequalities. The electricity crisis extends beyond urban centres. Rural areas often experience more severe and prolonged outages due to less developed infrastructure and slower response times. For instance, in the Free State, communities have faced not only load-shedding but also complete blackouts due to failing grid infrastructure. The pervasive impact of these outages highlights a broader governance and management failure within the national power sector.

The collapse of waste collection services in South Africa is another facet of the nationwide service delivery crisis. Across many municipalities, uncollected trash accumulates, creating severe health hazards and contributing to environmental degradation. Despite the presence of credentialed professionals within local governments, waste management remains ineffective, characterised by mismanagement and a lack of accountability. This failure disproportionately impacts the black majority in densely populated townships and informal settlements, where uncollected waste exacerbates pollution and illegal dumping, posing significant public health risks. The breakdown is evident in cities like Durban, where strikes by waste collection workers have led to mountains of garbage piling up on streets. In the Western Cape, the City of Cape Town has struggled with waste management disruptions due to financial constraints and logistical challenges. These issues are not confined to urban centres; rural municipalities also suffer from inadequate waste services, often resulting in illegal dumping and contamination of local water sources.

The collapse of municipal services across South Africa reflects profound governance failures at local, provincial, and national levels. From uncollected waste and frequent power outages to persistent water shortages, the inability to ensure effective service delivery has critically undermined public trust and confidence in the democratic system. Credentialed professionals at the helm of these services have frequently failed to address the crises, exposing the limitations of formal education in producing capable and ethical public servants. These failures are indicative of systemic issues in public administration and governance. The reliance on formal credentials has not translated into the practical skills and integrity required for effective public service delivery. The resulting governance issues have led to a vicious cycle of poor service delivery, diminished public trust, and increased social and economic inequalities.

5.5. The Unkept Promises of a Rainbow Nation: A Crisis of Competence and Consequences for the Youth

South Africa's systemic failures in healthcare and municipal services, despite the presence of credentialed professionals, are not isolated incidents but a reflection of deeper societal issues. The overemphasis on formal qualifications, coupled with a neglect of practical skills and ethical leadership, has created a breeding ground for incompetence, corruption, and mismanagement.

The consequences of these failures are most acutely felt by the country's youth. They are the ones who have grown up witnessing the unfulfilled promises of a "rainbow nation," experiencing firsthand the devastating effects of collapsing infrastructure, inadequate healthcare, and unreliable services. The high unemployment rate among young people, coupled with the lack of opportunities for advancement, further compounds their disillusionment.

The well-intentioned policies of affirmative action, while aimed at redressing historical injustices, have, in some instances, inadvertently contributed to these problems. By prioritizing demographics over merit in certain cases, the policy has inadvertently fueled resentment and undermined the principle of equality before the law. This has not only hindered the development of a truly meritocratic society but also deprived the nation of the best possible talent in crucial sectors.

The current generation of young South Africans, the very children who were meant to benefit from the new democratic dispensation, are instead bearing the brunt of its shortcomings. They are the ones who will inherit a nation grappling with a broken healthcare system, crumbling infrastructure, and a stagnant economy. This is not the future that was envisioned for them, nor is it the future they deserve.

As South Africa moves forward, it is imperative to acknowledge the unintended consequences of well-intentioned policies and to re-evaluate the overreliance on formal credentials. The focus must shift towards nurturing practical skills, fostering ethical leadership, and creating an environment where merit and competence are valued above all else. Only then can the nation hope to fulfil its promise of a better life for all its citizens, especially its youth.

Part III: The Legal Labyrinth

6. The Compass in the Labyrinth: The Best Interests of the Child in South African Law"

In the complex realm of child welfare and protection, the principle of "best interests of the child" serves as the guiding compass, illuminating the path through the intricate legal labyrinth. This fundamental tenet, enshrined in South African law, shapes the intricate web of legislation, institutions, and processes dedicated to safeguarding the well-being of the nation's most vulnerable members – its children.

The "best interests" principle is not merely an abstract concept; it is the paramount consideration in every decision, action, and legal proceeding affecting children. It serves as the unwavering beacon, ensuring that the rights, safety, and overall development of each child remain the focal point, transcending individual biases, societal norms, or institutional constraints.

This chapter aims to provide a comprehensive overview of the legal framework designed to uphold the best interests of the child, navigating the hierarchical structure of laws, institutions, and stakeholders involved in this critical endeavour.

6.1. The Foundation - The Constitution and the Best Interests Principle

The South African Constitution, the supreme law of the land, enshrines the rights of children in Section 28, laying the foundation for the legal system's commitment to their protection and well-being. This section not only guarantees fundamental rights such as the right to basic nutrition, shelter, basic health care services, and social services, but also establishes the "best interests" principle as the guiding light for all decisions affecting children.

6.2. The Legal Framework - Navigating the Levels

The legal framework governing child-related matters in South Africa is a complex, multi-layered structure, with each level playing a distinct yet interconnected role in upholding the best interests of the child.

At the apex of this hierarchy stands the South African Constitution, followed by key legislation such as the Children's Act, which operationalizes the constitutional principles and provides a comprehensive legal framework for addressing various aspects of child welfare, including parental rights and responsibilities, child protection, and alternative care.

> 6.2.1. **The High Court:** Occupying a unique position within this hierarchy is the High Court, designated as the "upper guardian" of all children. This esteemed institution bears the solemn responsibility of ensuring the welfare of minors and upholding the best interests principle, exercising oversight over lower courts and institutions involved in child-related matters.

> 6.2.2. **Children's Courts:** Dedicated tribunals known as Children's Courts play a pivotal role in adjudicating child custody, guardianship, and care proceedings. These specialised courts are bound by the Constitution and the Children's Act, and their rulings must prioritise the best interests of the child, taking into account various factors such as the child's physical, emotional, and developmental needs, as well as their social and cultural environment.

6.3. Department of Social Development: Social Workers and Family Advocates

Within the Department of Social Development, two key groups of professionals contribute to the realisation of the best interests principle:

6.3.1. **Social Workers:** These frontline advocates investigate child welfare concerns, conduct home visits, and prepare comprehensive reports for the courts, providing crucial insights into the child's circumstances and recommendations for their well-being.

6.3.2. **Family Advocates:** Serving as a neutral channel between conflicting parents, family advocates represent the voice of the child in legal proceedings, ensuring that the child's perspectives, needs, and best interests are considered throughout the decision-making process.

6.4. Working Together - Collaboration for the Child's Benefit

The legal framework governing child-related matters is not a collection of isolated entities; rather, it is a coordinated ecosystem in which the various stakeholders collaborate and interact to ensure the best interests of the child are met.

Social workers, family advocates, and legal representatives share information, submit reports, and provide testimony to inform the decisions of the Children's Courts. These courts, in turn, operate under the oversight of the High Court, which exercises its mandate as the upper guardian to ensure compliance with constitutional principles and the preservation of children's rights.

This interconnectivity and continuous exchange of information, expertise, and perspectives contribute to informed decision-making, where the child's voice is amplified, and their holistic well-being is the paramount consideration.

The principle of the best interests of the child serves as the compass that guides the legal labyrinth of child-related cases in South Africa. It is a beacon that illuminates the path for all stakeholders, institutions, and processes involved in the intricate web of child welfare and protection.

While this chapter provides an overview of the legal framework and its hierarchical structure, subsequent chapters in Part II will delve deeper into specific aspects of this complex system, exploring the nuances, challenges, and potential areas for reform.

Ultimately, the unwavering commitment to upholding the best interests of the child is not merely a legal obligation; it is a moral imperative that reflects the values of a society that prioritises the well-being and future of its most precious members.

7. The High Court's Guardianship: Protector of Children's Rights and Well-Being

In South Africa's pursuit of upholding the rights and safeguarding the welfare of its most vulnerable citizens, the nation's high court stands as an unwavering guardian – a resolute protector of the best interests of every child within its borders. The Constitution of South Africa has bestowed upon the High Court a unique and sacred mandate, one that transcends the confines of individual cases and extends to the broader realm of upholding the spirit and intent of the nation's foundational principles.

As the embodiment of judicial authority, the High Court is entrusted with the solemn duty of ensuring that the rights and well-being of children are upheld with the utmost diligence, regardless of their circumstances or backgrounds. This mandate is rooted in the principles of justice, equality, and an unwavering commitment to safeguarding the best interests of the nation's youngest and most vulnerable members of society.

Through this chapter, we will delve into the intricate web of responsibilities, oversight mechanisms, and accountability measures that empower the High Court to serve as the ultimate protector of children's rights and the arbiter of their best interests. From its constitutional foundations to its far-reaching influence over public and private entities, as well as professionals involved in child welfare, we will explore the multifaceted approach employed by the High Court to uphold its sacred duty.

7.1. Constitutional Foundations and Legal Authority

Section 28 of the Bill of Rights in the South African Constitution enshrines a comprehensive set of rights specifically designed to protect and uphold the well-being of children. This section serves as the foundation upon which the nation's commitment to safeguarding the interests of its most vulnerable members is built.

Section 28 of the South African Constitution specifically enumerates several crucial rights to safeguard children's well-being and development. These include the right to a name and nationality from birth, the assurance of family or parental care, or suitable alternative care if removed from the family environment. Children are also entitled to basic necessities such as nutrition, shelter, health care services, and social services. Additionally, they are protected from maltreatment, neglect, abuse, degradation, exploitative labour practices, and any work that is unsuitable for their age or detrimental to their health and development.

> 7.1.1. **Enumerated Rights:** Section 28 of the South African Constitution specifically enumerates several crucial rights to safeguard children's well-being and development. These include the right to a name and nationality from birth, the assurance of family or parental care, or suitable alternative care if removed from the family environment. Children are also entitled to basic necessities such as nutrition, shelter, health care services, and social services. Additionally, they are protected from maltreatment, neglect, abuse, degradation, exploitative labour practices, and any work that is unsuitable for their age or detrimental to their health and development.

> 7.1.2. **The Best Interests Principle:** Beyond these specific rights, Section 28(2) establishes the guiding principle known as the "best interests of the child" principle, stating:

> *"A child's best interests are of paramount importance in every matter concerning the child."*

This provision enshrines the fundamental principle that in all decisions, actions, and legal proceedings affecting children, their best interests must be the primary consideration, taking precedence over any other factors or competing interests.

7.1.3. Implications for the Legal Framework: The Constitution's emphasis on the best interests of the child has profound implications for the legal framework governing child-related matters in South Africa. It serves as the foundation upon which subsequent legislation, such as the Children's Act, and institutional mechanisms, including the High Court's role as the upper guardian, are built.

7.2. The High Court's Constitutional Mandate

The High Court's role as the ultimate protector of children's interests and the guardian of their best interests is firmly rooted in the constitutional mandate bestowed upon it. The Constitution empowers the High Court with the solemn responsibility of upholding the rights and well-being of children, transcending the boundaries of individual cases.

7.2.1. Multifaceted Mandate: The High Court's constitutional mandate is multifaceted, extending beyond the adjudication of individual cases to the broader realm of upholding the spirit and intent of the Constitution. The court is entrusted with ensuring that the principles enshrined in Section 28, including the paramount consideration of the child's best interests, are upheld and enforced across all spheres of society.

7.2.2. Ultimate Arbiter of Children's Interests: This mandate empowers the High Court to act as the ultimate arbiter of children's interests, transcending the confines of legal proceedings and extending its influence over the intricate web of institutions, processes, and stakeholders involved in shaping the outcomes of child-related matters.

7.2.3. Duties and Responsibilities as the Upper Guardian: As the designated upper guardian of all minor children within South Africa's borders, the High Court assumes a multifaceted array of duties and responsibilities rooted in ensuring that every decision, action, and legal proceeding involving children is conducted with the utmost regard for their best interests.

7.2.4. Oversight and Accountability Mechanisms: Central to the High Court's mandate is the establishment and maintenance of robust oversight and accountability mechanisms to ensure that all stakeholders involved in child-related matters prioritise the well-being of children above all else.

7.2.5. Upholding Fundamental Principles: The High Court's role extends beyond legal proceedings, encompassing a broader responsibility to uphold the principles of non-discrimination, equality before the law, and the preservation of fundamental rights for children across all spheres of society.

7.2.6. Proactive Approach: Fulfilling its duties as the upper guardian requires a proactive approach, a willingness to intervene and rectify any deviations from constitutional principles or instances where the rights and best interests of children are compromised.

7.2.7. Amplifying Children's Voices: Moreover, the High Court's guardianship extends to the promotion and protection of children's voices, ensuring that their perspectives, needs, and best interests are heard, considered, and respected throughout decision-making processes that shape their lives.

To effectively carry out its sacred duty as the guardian of children's rights and well-being, the High Court employs a comprehensive array of oversight mechanisms and accountability measures. These tools not only promote compliance with the best interests principle but also foster transparency, public trust, and a continuous pursuit of excellence in safeguarding the most vulnerable members of society. The following section will delve into the High Court's oversight mechanisms for entities, professionals, and the enforcement of ethical codes and professional standards.

7.3. Oversight Mechanisms for Entities

In recognition of the intricate web of public and private entities involved in matters concerning children's rights and well-being, the High Court has established comprehensive oversight mechanisms to ensure compliance with constitutional principles and the unwavering prioritisation of the best interests of the child. These oversight mechanisms are crucial in maintaining the integrity and accountability of the various institutions and organisations that shape the outcomes of child-related matters.

7.4. Oversight of Public Entities

The High Court, as the upper guardian of children, maintains strict oversight of Children's Courts and the Department of Social Development. This includes reviewing Children's Court decisions, ensuring they uphold the best interests of the child, and monitoring the conduct and performance of both courts and social workers. This multi-layered supervision is crucial in safeguarding the rights and well-being of children caught in legal proceedings or under the care of the state.

7.4.1. Children's Courts

At the forefront of the High Court's oversight responsibilities are the Children's Courts, specialised tribunals dedicated to adjudicating matters of child custody, guardianship, and care proceedings. These courts operate under the direct supervision of the High Court, which serves as the appellate body, reviewing decisions made by the Children's Courts to ensure adherence to constitutional principles and the best interests standard.

The High Court's oversight role in relation to the Children's Courts is multifaceted. Not only does it have the authority to review and, if necessary, overturn decisions that deviate from the principles of the Constitution or fail to prioritise the child's best interests, but it also plays a crucial role in monitoring the overall performance and conduct of these specialised tribunals.

Through periodic evaluations, audits, and performance reviews, the High Court can identify areas of concern, address systemic issues, and provide guidance to ensure that the Children's Courts consistently uphold the highest standards of due process, fairness, and child-centricity in their decision-making.

7.4.2. Department of Social Development

The High Court's oversight extends to the Department of Social Development, a crucial government agency responsible for the welfare and protection of children. In this capacity, the court closely monitors the performance and conduct of social workers employed by the department, ensuring that their investigations, home visits, and reports prioritise the well-being of children.

Social workers play a pivotal role in providing the courts with critical information and recommendations regarding child welfare cases. Their assessments and reports can significantly influence the outcomes of legal proceedings involving children. As such, the High Court's oversight of the Department of Social Development is essential to ensure that social workers maintain the highest standards of professionalism, objectivity, and a steadfast commitment to the best interests of the child.

Through regular performance reviews, the High Court can identify and address any lapses in the quality or impartiality of social workers' assessments, ensuring that their recommendations are grounded in rigorous analysis, factual evidence, and a child-centric approach rather than personal biases or institutional pressures.

7.5. Oversight of Private Entities

The High Court's role as the upper guardian of children extends beyond public entities, reaching into the private sector to ensure the well-being of children involved in legal proceedings and those residing in private care facilities.

7.5.1. Legal Firms and Practitioners

The High Court's oversight extends beyond public entities to encompass private legal firms and practitioners representing clients in child-related cases. As the guardian of children's rights and the arbiter of their best interests, the High Court has the authority to review the conduct of legal professionals engaged in these matters.

This oversight is crucial in ensuring that legal practitioners uphold the highest ethical standards and prioritise the well-being of children above all other considerations, including their clients' personal interests or financial incentives. The High Court's oversight serves as a check against potential conflicts of interest, unethical practices, or any actions that may compromise the best interests of the child.

In cases where legal professionals fail to uphold these standards or engage in conduct that violates the principles of child welfare, the High Court has the power to take disciplinary action. This may include issuing reprimands, suspensions, or, in severe cases, disbarment from practising law, reinforcing the court's commitment to maintaining the integrity of the legal profession and protecting the rights of children.

7.5.2. Private Care Facilities

The High Court's oversight extends to private institutions and facilities that provide care and accommodation for children, such as orphanages, foster homes, and residential care centres. In this domain, the court plays a crucial role in reviewing licensing procedures, operational standards, and the overall quality of care provided by these facilities.

Through regular inspections, audits, and investigations, the High Court can ensure that private care facilities comply with all relevant regulations, maintain appropriate living conditions, and prioritise the physical, emotional, and developmental well-being of the children under their care.

The High Court's oversight in this area is particularly important given the vulnerability of children in these facilities, many of whom may have experienced trauma, abuse, or neglect. By maintaining rigorous oversight, the court can identify and address any lapses in care, inadequate living conditions, or potential violations of children's rights, taking appropriate corrective measures to safeguard the well-being of these vulnerable individuals.

7.6. Oversight Mechanisms for Professionals: Admission and Registration

Recognizing the pivotal role played by various professionals in shaping the outcomes of child-related matters, the High Court has implemented robust oversight mechanisms to ensure that those entrusted with making decisions impacting children's lives possess the necessary qualifications, ethical standards, and an unwavering commitment to upholding the best interests principle. These oversight mechanisms are designed to maintain the integrity and competence of the legal and child welfare professions, fostering public trust and confidence in the systems that govern the well-being of South Africa's youngest and most vulnerable citizens.

7.6.1. Legal Practitioners

One of the High Court's fundamental oversight responsibilities is the admission and registration of legal practitioners in South Africa. All attorneys, advocates, and legal professionals must undergo a rigorous vetting process by the High Court before being granted the privilege of practising law within the nation's borders.

This admission process serves as a critical safeguard, ensuring that only individuals who possess the necessary qualifications, ethical standards, and a demonstrated commitment to upholding the principles of justice and the rule of law are permitted to represent clients in legal matters, including those involving children.

The High Court's vetting process for legal practitioners is comprehensive, encompassing an evaluation of academic credentials, professional experience, and ethical conduct. Candidates are carefully scrutinised to ensure that they possess the requisite knowledge, skills, and moral character to navigate the complexities of the legal system, particularly in matters pertaining to child welfare.

By exercising strict oversight in the admission of legal practitioners, the High Court aims to maintain the highest standards of professionalism within the legal field, fostering public confidence in the individuals entrusted with advocating for the rights and best interests of children in legal proceedings.

7.6.2. Prosecutors, Magistrates, and Judges

The High Court's oversight extends to the appointment and ongoing supervision of prosecutors, magistrates, and judges, including those presiding over Children's Courts and other tribunals adjudicating child-related matters. This oversight is crucial in ensuring that the individuals entrusted with interpreting and upholding the law possess the necessary impartiality, integrity, and unwavering commitment to the principles of justice and the best interests of the child.

In the appointment process for these critical roles, the High Court employs rigorous vetting procedures to assess candidates' qualifications, legal acumen, and ethical conduct. This evaluation aims to identify individuals who not only possess the requisite legal knowledge and experience but also demonstrate a deep understanding of the unique challenges and sensitivities involved in child welfare cases.

Once appointed, prosecutors, magistrates, and judges remain under the High Court's ongoing supervision, subject to performance reviews, audits, and accountability measures. This oversight is designed to ensure that these legal professionals continue to uphold the highest standards of impartiality, fairness, and a steadfast commitment to the best interests of the child in their decision-making processes.

7.6.3. Family Advocates

The Office of the Family Advocate plays a crucial role in representing the interests of children in legal proceedings, serving as a neutral and impartial voice advocating for the well-being of minors. Given the importance of this role, the High Court exercises direct oversight over the Office of the Family Advocate, including the performance and conduct of individual Family Advocates.

The High Court's oversight in this domain encompasses the appointment and registration of Family Advocates, ensuring that only qualified and ethical individuals are entrusted with this vital responsibility. Additionally, the court maintains ongoing supervision over the Office of the Family Advocate, monitoring their performance, investigating any complaints or concerns, and taking appropriate disciplinary action when necessary.

Through this comprehensive oversight, the High Court aims to ensure that Family Advocates consistently prioritise the best interests of children, advocating tirelessly for their rights, safety, and well-being throughout legal proceedings.

This oversight serves as a safeguard against any potential conflicts of interest, unethical conduct, or lapses in professional judgement that could compromise the integrity of the Family Advocate's role.

7.7. Oversight Mechanisms for Professionals: Ethical Codes and Professional Standards

Beyond mere admission and registration processes, the High Court plays a crucial role in enforcing ethical codes and professional standards that prioritise the best interests of the child. These codified guidelines serve as a moral compass, ensuring that all professionals involved in child-related matters uphold the highest standards of conduct and an unwavering commitment to child welfare. By maintaining oversight over these ethical frameworks, the High Court reinforces the principles of accountability, integrity, and a steadfast dedication to protecting the rights and well-being of South Africa's youngest and most vulnerable citizens.

7.7.1. Code of Conduct for Legal Practitioners

One of the High Court's key responsibilities is the enforcement of the Code of Conduct for Legal Practitioners, a comprehensive set of ethical guidelines governing the professional conduct of attorneys, advocates, and legal professionals in South Africa. This Code includes specific provisions related to representing clients in matters involving children, emphasising the paramount importance of upholding the best interests of the child.

7.7.2. The High Court's role in enforcing this Code of Conduct is multifaceted.

Not only does the court have the authority to investigate and adjudicate complaints of professional misconduct, but it also plays a proactive role in promoting adherence to these ethical standards through education, guidance, and ongoing oversight.

Violations of the Code of Conduct for Legal Practitioners, particularly in cases involving child welfare, can result in disciplinary actions imposed by the High Court. These actions may include reprimands, suspensions, or, in severe cases, disbarment from practising law. By taking a firm stance against unethical conduct, the High Court reinforces the importance of ethical behaviour and the prioritisation of the child's best interests in all legal proceedings.

7.7.3. Continuing Legal Education

In addition to enforcing ethical codes, the High Court plays a crucial role in promoting continuous professional development and education for legal practitioners. Through its oversight powers, the court may mandate continuing legal education requirements, ensuring that attorneys, advocates, and other legal professionals remain up-to-date with the latest developments in child welfare law, best practices, and emerging trends in the field.

These ongoing educational initiatives not only enhance the legal professionals' knowledge and expertise but also serve to reinforce the importance of ethical conduct, cultural sensitivity, and a steadfast commitment to upholding the best interests of the child. By fostering a culture of continuous learning and professional growth, the High Court aims to cultivate a legal profession that is well-equipped to navigate the complexities of child-related cases with the utmost competence, compassion, and a child-centric approach.

7.7.4. Codes of Conduct for Other Professionals

The High Court's oversight extends beyond the legal profession, encompassing various codes of conduct and professional standards applicable to other professionals involved in child-related matters. These include codes of conduct for magistrates presiding over Children's Courts, ethical guidelines for Family Advocates, and professional standards for judges adjudicating cases involving child welfare.

By ensuring adherence to these ethical frameworks, the High Court aims to maintain the highest levels of professionalism, impartiality, and an unwavering commitment to the best interests of the child across all spheres of the legal and child welfare systems. This oversight reinforces the principles of accountability, integrity, and a child-centric approach, fostering public trust and confidence in the processes and institutions designed to protect the rights and well-being of South Africa's children.

7.8. Oversight Mechanisms and Accountability

In discharging its sacred duty as the guardian of children's rights and well-being, the High Court employs a comprehensive array of oversight mechanisms and accountability measures. These tools not only promote compliance with the best interests principle but also foster transparency, public trust, and a continuous pursuit of excellence in safeguarding the most vulnerable members of society. Through these mechanisms, the High Court reinforces its commitment to upholding the highest standards of integrity, competence, and unwavering dedication to the welfare of South Africa's children.

7.8.1. Complaints and Disciplinary Procedures

The High Court has established robust procedures for receiving and investigating complaints against legal practitioners, social workers, Family Advocates, and other professionals involved in child-related matters. These complaints can originate from various sources, including concerned parents, advocacy groups, or the court's own internal monitoring processes.

Upon receiving a complaint, the High Court initiates a thorough investigation to assess the validity and severity of the allegations. This investigation may involve gathering evidence, conducting interviews, and reviewing relevant documentation and case files. If the complaint is substantiated, the High Court has the authority to impose disciplinary actions commensurate with the nature and gravity of the misconduct.

These disciplinary actions can range from formal reprimands and mandated training to more severe measures, such as suspensions or disbarment, in cases of egregious misconduct or repeated violations. By maintaining a transparent and rigorous complaints process, the High Court not only holds professionals accountable for their actions but also reinforces public confidence in the integrity of the child welfare system.

7.8.2. Performance Reviews and Audits

To ensure continuous improvement and adherence to the best interests principle, the High Court conducts periodic performance reviews and audits of Children's Courts, the Office of the Family Advocate, and other relevant entities. These evaluations are designed to assess the overall performance, efficiency, and effectiveness of these institutions in upholding the rights and well-being of children.

During these reviews and audits, the High Court examines various aspects of the entity's operations, including case management processes, decision-making procedures, adherence to ethical guidelines, and the implementation of best practices. The court may also solicit feedback from stakeholders, such as parents, legal professionals, and child welfare organisations, to gain a comprehensive understanding of the entity's strengths and areas for improvement.

Based on the findings of these evaluations, the High Court can provide guidance, recommendations, and, if necessary, directives to address any identified deficiencies or areas of concern. These performance reviews and audits serve as a proactive measure, ensuring that the institutions entrusted with protecting children's interests continuously strive for excellence and remain aligned with the best interests principle.

7.8.3. Judicial Oversight and Appeals

As an appellate body, the High Court exercises judicial oversight over lower courts by reviewing cases involving children's rights and well-being. Through the appeals process, the court has the authority to correct errors, provide guidance, and ensure consistent application of the best interests standard across all levels of the judicial system.

In reviewing appeals, the High Court critically examines the lower court's decision-making process, scrutinising the application of legal principles, the consideration of relevant evidence, and the adherence to constitutional mandates. If the court identifies errors, flawed reasoning, or deviations from the best interests principle, it has the power to overturn or modify the lower court's ruling, setting a precedent for future cases and reinforcing the primacy of the child's well-being in legal proceedings.

7.9. Reflecting on the High Court's Performance as the Upper Guardian

On paper, the South African High Court possesses a comprehensive legal and constitutional framework empowering it to serve as the unwavering protector of children's rights and the arbiter of their best interests. Through robust oversight mechanisms, enforcement of ethical codes, and collaboration with stakeholders, the High Court has the tools and authority to ensure that the well-being of every child remains the paramount consideration across all spheres of society.

However, as South Africa's democracy reaches the milestone of 30 years in 2024, a critical evaluation of the High Court's performance as the upper guardian is warranted. The children born in 1994, who should have been nurtured and safeguarded under the High Court's guardianship, are now adults with children of their own. Their lived experiences and the socioeconomic realities they face raise pressing questions about the effectiveness of the High Court's discharge of its constitutional duties.

Has the High Court truly upheld its sacred mandate, ensuring that the rights and best interests of children have been prioritised above all else? Or has it fallen short, failing to intervene decisively in instances where discriminatory practices, such as the persistent application of the maternal preference rule in custody cases, have persisted despite their unconstitutionality?

The voices of fathers and advocacy groups, echoed by constitutional entities like the Commission for Gender Equality, have repeatedly highlighted the discriminatory provisions within the Children's Act that ultimately impact the well-being of children. The fact that legal challenges were necessary to remove such provisions, as exemplified by the recent case of Van Wyk and Others v Minister of Employment and Labour, underscores the High Court's apparent inaction or inadequate responses to systemic issues.

Furthermore, when one considers the socioeconomic conditions faced by a generation that should have been protected under the High Court's guardianship, the question of accountability becomes paramount. How can the High Court reconcile its role as the guardian of children's rights with the stark realities of high unemployment rates, crime levels exceeding those of war zones, and the tragic phenomenon of women being victimised by the very men who were raised as children by single mothers due to the court's endorsement of discriminatory practices against fathers?

These sobering indicators raise the spectre of whether the High Court should be charged with child neglect for its failure to effectively discharge its constitutional duty, consequently failing an entire generation of children who have now become the struggling adults of today.

It is important to acknowledge that the High Court's performance has been shaped by various challenges, including limited resources, institutional constraints, entrenched societal biases, and the consequences of corruption facilitated by affirmative action policies. However, these challenges cannot be used as excuses for inaction or complacency when the well-being of children is at stake.

As South Africa looks to the future, a comprehensive and impartial evaluation of the High Court's role as the upper guardian is imperative. This assessment must be grounded in empirical evidence, statistical data, and the lived experiences of those directly impacted by the High Court's decisions and actions.

Only through such a critical examination can South Africa identify areas for improvement, implement necessary reforms, and chart a path towards a future where the High Court truly embodies the ideals of justice, equality, and unwavering protection for the nation's most vulnerable members – its children.

The inquiry into the High Court's performance as the upper guardian will be the subject of subsequent works, delving deeper into the court's successes, failures, and the systemic changes required to ensure that every child in South Africa has the opportunity to thrive, nurtured by the love, guidance, and support of both parents, free from the shackles of discrimination and inequality.

In the pursuit of a just and equitable society, the High Court's guardianship must be held to the highest standards, subject to continuous scrutiny and accountability. For it is only through such vigilance that the rights and well-being of children can truly be safeguarded, paving the way for a brighter future where every child's best interests are genuinely prioritised above all else.

GOLIATH'S RECKONING: UNVEILING THE BIASSED TRUTH BEHIND CHILDREN'S COURT THAT DISCRIMINATES AGAINST FATHERS

8. The Maternal Preference Rule and Its Impacts

The maternal preference rule and tender years doctrine have a long and complex history in South Africa, intertwined with the nation's colonial past and the evolution of its legal system. This chapter will examine the origins and impacts of these legal principles, their application to indigenous South African communities, and the significant shift brought about by the adoption of the new Constitution in 1994. We will explore how the equality clause rendered the maternal preference rule unconstitutional, and the ongoing societal consequences of its previous application, particularly for fathers, children, and perceptions of parenting roles.

8.1. Background of the Maternal Preference Rule and Tender Years Doctrine

The maternal preference rule and tender years doctrine are legal principles that have historically favoured mothers in child custody cases. The tender years doctrine, originating in English common law, presumes that young children, typically under the age of seven, should be placed in the care of their mothers. The maternal preference rule extends this presumption, giving preference to mothers in custody disputes even for older children.

These doctrines were rooted in traditional gender roles and the belief that mothers were inherently better nurturers and caregivers than fathers. They reflected and reinforced societal expectations of women as primary caregivers and men as breadwinners, with limited involvement in child-rearing.

8.1.1. Application in South Africa

South Africa's legal system, shaped by its colonial history, incorporated elements of English common law, including the tender years doctrine and maternal preference rule. These principles were applied in custody cases, often resulting in mothers being granted custody even when fathers were equally or better suited to care for the children.

However, the application of these doctrines failed to account for the diverse child-rearing practices of South Africa's indigenous communities. Among the Xhosa and Khoisan peoples, for example, child-rearing was often a communal responsibility, with extended family and community members playing significant roles. The rigid mother-centric approach of the maternal preference rule and tender years doctrine was not always aligned with these traditional practices.

8.1.2. The Constitutional Shift in Parenting Equality in South Africa

The adoption of South Africa's democratic Constitution marked a significant turning point. The Constitution's equality clause (Section 9) prohibits unfair discrimination on various grounds, including gender. This, coupled with the principle of the best interest of the child, rendered the maternal preference rule and tender years doctrine unconstitutional, as they inherently discriminated against fathers based on their sex.

Under the equality clause, any discrimination based on the listed grounds is presumed to be unfair unless proven otherwise. In the context of the maternal preference rule, there are no justifiable grounds for discrimination. The assumption that mothers are inherently better caregivers simply by virtue of their gender is baseless and perpetuates harmful stereotypes. While some mothers, like my own, have dedicated their lives to child-rearing as a career and have developed exceptional parenting skills, it is wrong to assume that all women are inherently better parents simply because of their gender.

If we were to accept the notion that women are naturally superior caregivers, then the same logic should apply to other areas of life, such as voting rights, education, and employment. However, this is not the case. In fact, not only is there equality before the law when it comes to recruitment, but there are also affirmative action policies that actively discriminate against boys and men to ensure that girls and women are never discriminated against in the formal school and workplace.

The inconsistency in applying the concept of gender-based superiority highlights the flawed reasoning behind the maternal preference rule. If women are not automatically assumed to be better voters, students, or employees due to their gender, then it is unjust to presume that they are inherently better caregivers.

Moreover, the presence of affirmative action policies that favour women in various spheres of life demonstrates the recognition that gender alone does not determine one's abilities or qualifications. These policies aim to counteract historical and systemic discrimination against women, acknowledging that gender-based discrimination is unacceptable and that individual merit should be the primary consideration.

By applying the same principles to parenting, it becomes clear that the maternal preference rule is not only unconstitutional but also inconsistent with the values of equality and non-discrimination enshrined in the Constitution. Fathers should not be subjected to unfair discrimination based on their gender, and the determination of parental rights and responsibilities should be based on a case-by-case assessment of each parent's capacity, commitment, and the best interests of the child.

The Constitution's equality clause, together with the principle of the best interest of the child, serves as powerful tools to challenge and dismantle discriminatory practices like the maternal preference rule. By ensuring that both parents are evaluated on their individual merits and capabilities, South Africa can uphold the values of equality and non-discrimination that are foundational to its legal system.

8.2. Impact of systematic discrimination against fathers.

8.2.1. Impact on Children: The Detrimental Consequences

The application of the maternal preference rule, as has been the case for other state-entrenched discrimination in affirmative action, has had the worst consequences for children. This is no more evident than in the current socio-economic status of the country. The children who were born in 1994, who ought to have benefited from post-apartheid South Africa, are now languishing as adults with high unemployment, failing quality of service at every level, from an education system that failed to equip them with the skills they need as adults to a health sector that is crumbling like every government and municipal service in most of the country.

8.2.2. Denying Children the Benefits of Equal Parenting

By prioritising maternal custody, the rule denies the child the benefit of being raised by both parents. It is not a coincidence that for a child to be conceived, two people of the opposite sex are a prerequisite. Far more important than the material and economic benefits of shared labour when both parents are treated equally, the biggest benefit to the child of having both parents involved is that the child can learn more about themselves from both the parents and members of the extended family, as each of them has genetic links to the child. Some of the traits and characteristics that are likely to manifest in the child as a consequence of genes already manifest in the family members, from parents to the extended kin. This means the child can learn about themselves fully by observing other people who share the same genes as them.

8.2.3. The Trauma of Parental Loss and Unfamiliarity

The consequences of unequal parenting rights are even worse in the case of the worst-case scenario, where either the mother or both parents die. The denial of equal parenting rights means that the child often knows and attaches to only one parent or parent's family. This means that in addition to the stress of having to deal with the loss of a parent, the child now must adjust to the parent they never knew, in new surroundings, all of which add further strain to the grieving child. The younger the child gets to know their parents and living circumstances, the quicker they can acclimate to both, form solid emotional attachments with both parents and extended family members. In case of the demise of one of the parents, the child mostly has to deal with the grief of the parent, but knowing that at least they still have the same security in the other parent in an environment that they are familiar with because the child spent adequate time with both parents. Should this be worse and both parents die, the child will still be far better off because since they spent adequate time with both parents, they are likely to have a relationship with their extended family members with whom they would most likely end up. This is far much better than having to meet the new family for the first time with no prior relationship.

8.2.4. Undervaluing the Importance of Fathers

Furthermore, the maternal preference rule has reinforced the notion that children primarily need their mothers, undervaluing the importance of fathers in children's lives. This can strain father-child relationships and deprive children of the unique contributions and perspectives that fathers offer. Children benefit from the diverse experiences, skills, and emotional support that both mothers and fathers bring to their lives. By perpetuating the idea that mothers are inherently better suited to childcare, the maternal preference rule not only undermines the role of fathers but also limits the potential for children to develop well-rounded personalities and a healthy understanding of gender roles.

As a man, my father was my benchmark. Until I surpassed his greatest achievements, I felt I was a failure, mediocre at best. Thankfully, the time I had with him, though short, was enough for me to learn and grow. He taught me, directly and indirectly, to build upon his legacy and strive for more, just as he had done with the lessons passed down from his father. To truly understand my father and his aspirations, I immersed myself in his world, spending time with him and his family.

Even after his passing, my mother, often against my own wishes, insisted I maintain close ties with his side of the family, just as I did with hers. It was through this holistic understanding of both my parents and their families that I gained a deeper understanding of myself. This self-awareness empowered me to not only follow in my father's footsteps but to exceed his accomplishments and provide for his family beyond his dreams. By understanding him, I could amplify his strengths and learn from his shortcomings.

8.2.5. The Need for Equal Parenting Rights

To address these issues and ensure the best interests of children, it is essential to challenge the maternal preference rule and advocate for equal parenting rights. This involves recognizing the importance of both parents in a child's life, regardless of their marital status or gender. By promoting shared parenting arrangements and encouraging the active involvement of both mothers and fathers, South Africa can create a more supportive and nurturing environment for children to grow and thrive.

Furthermore, in cases where one or both parents are deceased, having established relationships with both sides of the family can provide children with a vital sense of continuity, belonging, and emotional support during a challenging time. By fostering these connections from an early age, children can develop the resilience and adaptability needed to navigate life's uncertainties.

Ultimately, the well-being and development of children should be the primary consideration in all custody and parenting arrangements. By dismantling the maternal preference rule and promoting equal parenting rights, South Africa can take a significant step towards creating a society that truly values the best interests of its children and recognizes the essential contributions of both mothers and fathers in their lives.

8.3. Impact on Fathers

The application of the maternal preference rule has had lasting impacts on fathers in South Africa. By presuming mothers to be the preferred custodial parent, the rule has reinforced the notion that fathers are secondary or less important in their children's lives. This has discouraged many fathers from seeking custody or actively participating in child-rearing.

8.3.1. Unequal Starting Point

Under South African law, mothers automatically receive full parental rights and responsibilities upon a child's birth, regardless of marital status or level of involvement in the child's life. While married fathers also have these rights, many fathers feel pressured to acquiesce to their wives' wishes to avoid court battles, perceiving a bias against them in the legal system. This leaves fathers, both married and unmarried, vulnerable to the mother's decisions regarding the child.

In contrast, fathers must actively pursue legal recognition to secure their parental rights, often facing significant obstacles. This inherent inequality disadvantages fathers from the start. Additionally, should a father wish to exercise his constitutional rights, the law imposes additional burdens on him that mothers do not face.

This disparity raises concerns about fairness and equal treatment for both parents in matters of child custody and parental rights.

8.3.2. Unlawful Deprivation and Potential Kidnapping

In many cases, mothers exploit this legal bias to withhold children from their fathers without their consent. This act, which can be interpreted as parental child abduction or even kidnapping, is often facilitated or endorsed by the children's court itself. By issuing orders that prioritise the mother's wishes over the father's rights and the child's best interests, the court may be complicit in a criminal act.

8.3.3. The Unequal Burden of Proof on Fathers

For a father to gain his equal right to discharge his obligations to the child, the law imposes additional steps that are not required of the mother. The father must first apply to a court, which then triggers the involvement of the family advocate, who conducts an assessment and issues a report to the court. This process is reminiscent of the historical struggle for women's suffrage. Imagine if, after decades of fighting for the right to vote, which in most countries was initially confined to certain men of certain status but ultimately extended to all men, women finally won the right to vote but with the following stipulations:

"Henceforth, like every man, women will be deemed equal under the law and can vote just like men. However, for a woman to vote, she must pay a fee and pass an assessment to confirm she is as fit to vote as men are. Since men have been voting since time immemorial, there is no need for them to pay this fee or undergo an assessment, but for women, it is a prerequisite."

This scenario is analogous to the situation faced by fathers who wish to exercise their constitutional rights, a practice not only normalised in children's courts but also documented in the Children's Act.

8.3.4. Hindering the Breakdown of Traditional Gender Roles

The maternal preference rule has significantly impacted the transition of men into domestic roles. By perpetuating the notion that child-rearing primarily belongs to women, this rule has hindered progress toward equal sharing of parenting responsibilities and the breakdown of traditional gender norms. Unfortunately, this not only deprives children of the opportunity to benefit from the full involvement of both parents but also reinforces harmful stereotypes about mothers and fathers in family life.

However, let's delve deeper. The reality, unvarnished and essential, is that even exceptional women, like my mother who have succeeded in their child rearing careers owe part of their achievements to the support provided by men. Whether it's grandfathers, uncles, fathers, husbands or partners, men like me have played a crucial role in ensuring that the women we provided for and were obligated to, by choice, could excel in their chosen endeavours. Acknowledging this interconnectedness allows us to appreciate the collective effort that contributes to individual success

8.4. The Far-Reaching Impact of State-Sanctioned Discrimination on Mothers, Familial Relations, and Society

State-sanctioned discrimination in children's courts not only violates the principle of equality before the law but also results in strained familial relations. The application of the equality principle would mean that fathers need not go to extremes to prove what is their constitutional right, such that they have to prove their case beyond a reasonable doubt.

A magistrate told me directly that for her to grant custody to me as a man, the mother would have to be a drug addict or junkie, which means the standard for the best father is measured against the worst mothers. As a consequence of this, I now have to build a criminal case against the mother of my child, something which is both undesirable but has now become a necessity. I am not short of criminal acts she has conducted in trying to maintain her unconstitutional stance, which include lying in court claiming that I was violent towards her, using illegal immigrants as nannies to watch over her son, slander in front of a magistrate where she and her legal representative claimed I was a drunk and addict, as well as kidnapping, because for as long as she has exercised her right to our son beyond what is due to her, she infringed on mine and withheld my son from me against my will, which constitutes kidnapping.

8.4.1. The Negation of Merit and the Perpetuation of Complacency

The worst thing about this biassed approach is that it negates any merit because it doesn't matter how good a father is; by virtue of being a man, he is already at a disadvantage. Women, on the other hand, can be as complacent with their lives as they want, failing to take opportunities that are before them because they know that even if they do not make enough income to support themselves, they can just have a child and exploit the system to extort money from the father or man, either through maintenance or grants. The unfortunate thing about all this is that children learn from their parents. If the example set by the mother is that even if she doesn't do anything, she will be protected by the law, and the father will be punished, the child has no incentive to be a father when he grows up. The image he has is that by virtue of being a man, he is disadvantaged, and no matter what he does, it will count for little. What should have been a child that looks up to the good example of parents who work on themselves to improve their circumstances is negated by the perception of entitlement.

8.4.2. The Joy and Fulfilment of Raising a Family

I am not aware of anything that gives my mother, as a mother, more joy than raising her family. For all the hype about formal career achievements from academic pursuits or career achievements, they quickly diminish, but the joy of raising a child to an adult and playing a role in their grandchildren is a lifelong accomplishment. This means that a biassed stance automatically deprives paternal grandmothers, a form of female oppression. On the other hand, maternal grandmothers are burdened with responsibilities they may not necessarily want beyond what is acceptable, which is equal time in both parents' households for the child.

8.4.3. The Importance of Experience and Expertise in Child-Rearing

A grandmother who spent her life as a career woman with travelling achievements and goals is not going to suddenly morph into a domesticated career grandmother with a lifetime of skills and knowledge in child and grandchild rearing. This is exactly the case with my son's grandmothers.

While my mother, who is also the only one of the two to raise a man and has been a crucial part of grandsons older than my son, is now deprived of the opportunity to impart that knowledge, someone who not only lacks such a lifetime of expertise is suddenly burdened beyond what is reasonable with it. And if it must come to it, merit counts, and absolutely measured using objective measures like tax contributions, lifetime achievements, and the extent of skills that can be imparted to the child, there is no question that my mother in me is the more experienced and qualified.

8.4.4. The Insult of Discrimination Against Mothers

For all the accusations of women who opt to choose to raise their children as their sole career of them not having qualifications, when it comes down to it, I am my mother's highest qualification. But she does not have one, but my sisters as well, and now my nephews and niece. As much as I can tolerate an insult against me, I can never tolerate an insult against my mother, which is what this discrimination does!

8.4.5. The Need for Loyalty to the Constitution

It is also the same reverence for my own mother that I totally oppose the discrimination by children's courts against fathers because now I have to resort to extreme measures as far as criminal proceedings against the mother of my son, something which could have been avoided if the courts were loyal to the constitution they are supposed to uphold.

8.4.6. The Detrimental Impact of State-Sanctioned Discrimination on Society

State-sanctioned discrimination, whether on the basis of race or gender, is contrary to the equality principle but most conflicts with the best interests of the child. But for discrimination under the guise of redress, the adults who were children in 1994 would be having a better future today. Instead, they have to be judged based on their skin colour and gender, breeding more racial and gender tension in a country that was supposed to be a rainbow nation.

8.5. Societal Perceptions of Parenting

The maternal preference rule and tender years doctrine have shaped societal perceptions of parenting in South Africa. They have entrenched the notion of mothers as natural caregivers and fathers as peripheral figures in child-rearing. This has created barriers for fathers seeking to be more involved in their children's lives and has placed undue pressure on mothers to fulfil traditional caregiving roles.

Challenging these perceptions is crucial for promoting gender equality and recognizing the diverse ways in which families can thrive. It requires a shift towards valuing the contributions of both parents and making custody determinations based on the best interests of the child, rather than outdated gender stereotypes.

8.6. Conclusion

The maternal preference rule and tender years doctrine have cast a long shadow over South African society, deeply influencing family dynamics, gender roles, and perceptions of parenting. Despite the constitutional shift in 1994 that deemed these principles unconstitutional, their legacy lingers, perpetuating outdated gender stereotypes and disadvantaged fathers and children alike.

The ongoing impact of these doctrines is multifaceted. Children have borne the brunt of this systemic discrimination, often denied the balanced upbringing that comes from being raised by both parents.

The socio-economic struggles faced by post-apartheid generations highlight the broader consequences of such discriminatory practices. The rule's bias has deprived children of the genetic and emotional benefits of dual-parent involvement, forcing them to navigate life with a skewed understanding of family and self-identity. The trauma of losing a parent, compounded by unfamiliarity with the surviving parent or extended family, underscores the rule's detrimental impact on children's psychological well-being.

For fathers, the maternal preference rule has reinforced harmful stereotypes, positioning them as secondary figures in their children's lives. This not only strains father-child relationships but also discourages fathers from seeking custody or engaging actively in child-rearing. The unequal legal starting point for fathers, who must often undergo burdensome processes to gain parental rights, exemplifies the systemic bias that perpetuates inequality. The necessity for fathers to prove their capability to an extent not required of mothers creates an environment where paternal contributions are undervalued, and fathers are disempowered.

Moreover, the rule's impact extends to societal perceptions of parenting and gender roles. By enshrining mothers as primary caregivers, it has hindered the breakdown of traditional gender roles, preventing men from fully participating in domestic life. This not only limits the potential for children to benefit from diverse parental influences but also reinforces a societal structure that confines women to caregiving roles and men to economic ones.

The need for legal reform is paramount. Challenging the constitutionality of the maternal preference rule and advocating for amendments to the Children's Act are critical steps toward ensuring equal parenting rights. Removing the additional hurdles imposed on fathers and fostering a case-by-case approach to custody decisions, based on the child's best interests, would mark significant progress. Public awareness campaigns and educational initiatives can further dismantle the societal biases underpinning these doctrines, promoting a more balanced and inclusive view of parenting roles.

The far-reaching impact of state-sanctioned discrimination, whether based on gender or race, cannot be overstated. Such discrimination strains familial relations, negates merit, and perpetuates complacency, ultimately harming society. The legacy of the maternal preference rule serves as a poignant reminder of the importance of adhering to constitutional principles of equality and merit.

As a father, my journey underscores the critical need for a fair and just legal system that values the contributions of both parents. The joy and fulfilment of raising a family, the invaluable experience and expertise of grandmothers, and the importance of equal parenting rights are central to fostering a society that truly values the well-being and development of its children. By challenging discriminatory practices and promoting equal parenting, South Africa can create a more just and harmonious future, where the best interests of children are genuinely upheld, and both mothers and fathers are recognized as essential caregivers.

In conclusion, dismantling the maternal preference rule is not just a legal necessity but a societal imperative. By embracing true equality and recognizing the vital roles both parents play, we can build a society that fosters the growth and development of our children, free from the constraints of outdated and discriminatory practices.

9. Legal Presumptions and Their Application in the Children's Act

Legal presumptions are a fundamental concept in the South African legal system, playing a crucial role in guiding judicial decision-making and the allocation of rights and responsibilities. This chapter will explore the nature and purpose of legal presumptions, with a particular focus on rebuttable presumptions. We will examine how these presumptions apply within the realm of the Children's Act, in light of the equality clause enshrined in the Constitution. Specifically, we will discuss how the principle of equality before the law necessitates a rebuttable presumption of equal parental rights and responsibilities from the moment of a child's conception and birth.

9.1. Understanding Legal Presumptions: Conclusive and Rebuttable

Legal presumptions are fundamental rules that enable courts to assume certain facts as true based on the presence of other established facts. These rules are designed to streamline legal proceedings and enhance efficiency by eliminating the need for parties to prove every fact in a case. Presumptions in law can be classified into two main categories: conclusive and rebuttable.

- **Presumption of Innocence in Criminal Law:** One of the cornerstone principles in criminal justice is the presumption of innocence. This legal presumption mandates that the prosecution prove a defendant's guilt beyond a reasonable doubt. Until such proof is provided, the defendant is considered innocent. This presumption is critical in protecting the rights of the accused and ensuring that the state does not unjustly deprive any individual of liberty.

- **Marital Presumption of Paternity in Family Law:** Known formally as "pater est quem nuptiae demonstrant" (the husband is presumed to be the father), this rebuttable presumption applies when a child is born during a marriage. The law assumes that the husband of the mother is the child's biological father, streamlining paternity determinations and securing legal rights for the child from birth. This presumption, however, can be challenged with substantial evidence such as DNA testing. While there is a legal presumption that a child born to a married woman is the biological offspring of her husband, this presumption can be challenged through DNA testing if there is compelling evidence to the contrary.

For children born outside of marriage, paternity is not legally presumed. This allows putative fathers the opportunity to establish their biological relationship to the child through proper legal channels, if they wish to do so. Ultimately, every child deserves the chance to form a bond with their biological father and receive his care and support, assuming paternity is confirmed. DNA testing provides an objective scientific means to verify paternity while ensuring the child's best interests are upheld.

- **Presumption of Legitimacy:** This presumption holds that a child born during a marriage is legitimate. The law conclusively presumes the legality of the child's birth, which bears implications for inheritance rights and family status. Overturning this presumption typically requires strong legal evidence to the contrary.

- **Presumption of Death After Seven Years:** In situations where an individual disappears under circumstances where death is likely, but no body has been found, the law presumes death after seven years of continuous absence. This conclusive presumption allows families to settle estates and move forward with legal processes related to the deceased.

- **Presumption of Regularity:** This presumption asserts that official duties and procedures, such as those carried out by government officials, have been conducted properly and legally. It is conclusive, meaning that it provides public acts with a presumption of legality unless unequivocal evidence is presented.

- **Presumption of Sanitary Compliance:** In food safety regulations, there is a conclusive presumption that products manufactured in a facility complying with government standards are safe and sanitary. This presumption is crucial for public health protection but can be contested if evidence of non-compliance is demonstrated.

Conclusive presumptions are absolute and cannot be overturned by further evidence once the foundational facts are established. In contrast, rebuttable presumptions provide an initial assumption that can be contested; sufficient evidence presented by the opposing party can overturn these presumptions. This distinction is vital as it dictates the burden of proof dynamics in legal proceedings.

9.2. Rebuttable Presumptions in the Children's Act

In the context of the Children's Act, rebuttable presumptions play a significant role in determining parental rights and responsibilities. The Act aims to promote the best interests of the child and ensure that both parents have the opportunity to be involved in their child's life.

The equality clause in the Constitution guarantees equality before the law and prohibits unfair discrimination on various grounds, including gender. This constitutional principle has important implications for the application of rebuttable presumptions in the Children's Act.

9.3. Equal Parental Rights and Responsibilities

The equality clause mandates that both parents have equal rights and responsibilities in relation to their minor child, starting from the moment of conception and birth. This means that there is a rebuttable presumption of equal parental involvement, regardless of the parents' marital status or gender.

This presumption challenges historical gender stereotypes and the traditional allocation of parental roles. It recognizes that both mothers and fathers have the capacity and right to be actively involved in their child's upbringing, and that the child's best interests are served by having the love, care, and support of both parents.

9.4. Unconstitutionality of Burden of Proof on Fathers

In light of the equality clause, it is unconstitutional to place the burden of proof on fathers when they seek to enforce their equal rights and responsibilities. Requiring fathers to prove their suitability or competence as parents, while presuming mothers to be naturally suited for caregiving, perpetuates harmful gender stereotypes and undermines the principle of equality.

The rebuttable presumption of equal parental rights and responsibilities should apply equally to both parents. Any deviation from this presumption must be justified by compelling evidence that it is in the best interests of the child. The onus should be on the party seeking to limit or restrict a parent's involvement to prove that such a limitation is necessary and proportionate.

9.5. Constitutional Impact & Rebuttable Presumption of Equal Rights and Responsibilities

The South African Constitution, specifically Section 9 which prohibits unfair discrimination based on sex, has significantly impacted child custody matters. This section establishes a rebuttable presumption that both biological parents hold equal rights and responsibilities towards their child, born after the Constitution came into effect in 1994.

Previously, the legal system often favoured mothers in custody disputes through the "maternal preference rule." However, Section 9 of the Bill of Rights renders this practice unconstitutional. This principle was further solidified in the landmark case of Hugo v Hugo (2003) [You can insert the citation for the case here if you have it].

This rebuttable presumption creates a shift in the burden of proof. When a father seeks equal rights and responsibilities, the onus doesn't fall on him to prove his claim. Instead, the burden lies with the party contesting his involvement.

However, it's important to note a nuance. If a father desires full custody, the burden shifts back to him. He must then demonstrate that the mother is unfit to share parental duties. In all other situations, where the father seeks equal rights and shared parenting, the Constitution grants him this right automatically based on the presumption of equal parental involvement.

This legal framework ensures fairer treatment for fathers and prioritises the best interests of the child by encouraging active participation from both parents.

9.6. Legislation Supporting Equal Parental Rights and Responsibilities

The South African Constitution establishes the foundation for equal parental rights, but numerous laws further reinforce this principle. Here's how key pieces of legislation work in tandem:

- **The Promotion of Equality and Prevention of Unfair Discrimination Act (PEPUDA)**: Building on the Constitution's anti-discrimination clause, PEPUDA specifically prohibits discrimination based on gender. This strengthens the automatic rebuttable presumption of equal rights and responsibilities for biological parents towards their child.

- **The Children's Act (Act 38 of 2005)**: This Act directly addresses parental roles and responsibilities.

  ○ Section 18: It emphasises the principle that both parents share parental responsibilities and rights regarding their child's care, education, and well-being. This reinforces the rebuttable presumption established by the Constitution.

  ○ Section 21: This section outlines the best interests of the child as the primary consideration in all matters concerning them. In determining custody and access arrangements, courts must consider factors that promote a meaningful relationship with both parents, unless there's evidence demonstrating harm to the child.

The Children's Act, combined with PEPUDA, creates a legal framework that discourages courts from favouring one parent based solely on gender. This ensures that fathers, just like mothers, have the opportunity to establish a strong and nurturing bond with their children. These legislative measures have a significant impact on child custody arrangements in South Africa.

Fathers now have a stronger legal footing to claim equal rights and responsibilities, removing the historical bias towards mothers. This promotes shared parenting arrangements, which research suggests can benefit children by providing them with the love and support of both parents.

It's important to remember that the presumption of equal rights is rebuttable. If compelling evidence demonstrates that one parent poses a risk to the child's well-being, the court can deviate from this principle. However, the burden of proof lies with the party contesting equal involvement.

9.7. Conclusion

Legal presumptions, particularly rebuttable presumptions, play a vital role in the application of the Children's Act in South Africa. The equality clause in the Constitution necessitates a rebuttable presumption of equal parental rights and responsibilities from the moment of a child's conception and birth.

This presumption challenges historical gender biases and promotes a more equitable approach to parenting. It is unconstitutional to place the burden of proof on fathers when they seek to enforce their equal rights and responsibilities, as this undermines the principle of equality before the law.

By embracing the rebuttable presumption of equal parental involvement, the Children's Act can foster gender equality, support the best interests of children, and create a legal framework that recognizes and values the contributions of both mothers and fathers. This shift towards equal parenting is essential for building a society where gender stereotypes are dismantled, and children can thrive under the love and care of both parents.

Part IV: Unveiling the Bias

10. Acquiring Full Parental Rights and Responsibilities as a Biological Father in South Africa (A Step-by-Step Guide)

The legal process to acquire full parental rights and responsibilities as a biological father in South Africa is outlined in the Children's Act. While it is crucial for both parents and extended families to know what the law specifies, it is not desirable for the case to end up in a court of law.

Regardless of the short-term gains for the winning parent, the long-term consequences are borne by the child. Contrary to popular belief and advice from most legal representatives and judicial officers who profit from their services, there is seldom a win for a child from conflicting parents. The income that could otherwise contribute to the child's well-being is instead spent on protracted legal processes with decisions made by surrogates who have no long-term interest in the child's welfare.

10.1. The Importance of Parental Cooperation

Just as it takes two people to conceive a child, it is often best that the way they raise the child comes from the two people who were the prerequisites to the child's existence. Naturally, neither party knows better, especially if they are first-time parents who may be young, so disagreements are bound to happen.

Once the parents have discussed but couldn't reach an agreement, it is better to seek counsel from family members before going outside. External resources are crucial so that everyone is aware of the legal requirements, but in reality, these resources and legal instruments merely reinforce what ought to be logical when dealing with a child: it is not the parent's feelings that matter, but the best interest of the child that should take precedence.

10.2. Power Imbalances and the Role of the Law

Often, most people forget this and try to make the agreement about what they want, irrespective of the long-term considerations for the child. This is even more likely to happen in cases where there is a power imbalance, as is the case in South Africa with the pervasive bias of children's courts in favouring mothers while making fathers bear the financial costs in decisions relating to children's care.

Sometimes, even without the court's bias, the level of material well-being can swing the power balance between the parents towards the parent with the financial means to afford legal representation. This is why the principle of equality before the law is crucial because it is when these imbalances between the parents come into play that the parent who feels in an unequal position puts the matter before the court, where both parties are equal before the law, and it is the best interest of the child that will take precedence.

10.3. Exhausting Internal Resources

Until such time that the parents have exhausted all the internal resources within the family to try and reach an agreement, it is not advisable to default to the formal legal process. Often, during negotiations between the parents, there is a disagreement that is not necessarily adversarial but based on a misunderstanding or lack of knowledge of the law. In these cases, both parents can go to court or social workers to seek advice, in hopes that these entities will adhere to their professional code of conduct and be ethical in offering unbiased advice that is in the best interest of the child.

10.4. The Law's Focus on Amicable Agreements

The law's focus on achieving amicable agreements in relation to children is so pronounced that even in the code of ethics for legal practitioners, private legal practitioners are required to prioritise the best interest of the child in terms of rule 59.2 and make sure that the agreement they facilitate is equitable to both parties. This means that even if the outcome of the agreement might prejudice the parent who appointed the legal representative, rule 59.2 effectively means the legal representative has a primary obligation to the child and a secondary obligation to both parents rather than their client solely.

10.5. Preparing as a Father

Be prepared as a father once you have decided to have a child. Ideally, you want to plan this long before conception because it will take all your efforts and resources. You must know as much of the law as you can and be realistic about your expectations. Even though you might have a strong case, because of the bias of the judicial officers in the children's courts, you might still lose. Be prepared mentally and make sure to surround yourself with people you can count on for parenting advice, legal advice, medical advice, etc.

10.6. The Intention to Avoid Conflict

The intention to avoid conflict between the parents is so pronounced that even the children's court process deviates from normal open court processes. Unlike normal courts, children's court proceedings are held in private or are partially enclosed, and the judicial officer plays an active role in the proceedings.

While the application of these has fallen far short of the requirements, the reality is that the intention makes sense when one considers the stress and trauma of going to court for the parents. Rather than fight, it makes sense to cooperate because both parents have a direct stake. A win for one parent at the expense of the other ultimately takes away from the child. But if all efforts to reach an agreement amicably fail, the court process then needs to be applied.

10.7. Malicious Mothers and the Courts

While the prospect of a mother who would put her interests above those of her child is inconceivable to most of us who were raised by mothers who knew their duties in respect to their children, malicious mothers who seek to use their children to gain power over the father are more the norm than the exception.

This is even more likely to happen in a case where the man has more financial resources than the woman. Hypergamy explains this, but most women know they need not even bother with the marriage but get a child from the man in order to gain dominion over him.

This is facilitated by the courts who are biassed towards mothers and continue to apply the maternal preference rule as well as the tender years doctrine, despite these having been unconstitutional in South Africa since 1994. This injustice by the courts has created a victim mentality amongst immoral mothers because they know that irrespective of the merits of the father's case, the courts will side with them.

10.8. Private Legal Representatives and Bias

Private legal representatives have also noticed this court bias and have made sure to benefit from it. Contrary to their ethical obligations, they know they get easy clients from mothers and they advise them, even going as far as to fabricate lies under oath in order to get a restraining order against the father.

This strategy is meant to threaten the father into surrendering his rights and acquiescing to every decision the mother makes, irrespective of its merits or detriment to the child. Even within a marriage, a significant proportion of fathers are threatened by women to acquiesce because the mother tells the father that should he speak up or assert his equal rights, she will take him to court, which is likely to side with her.

She will use their kids to take all his assets, from the house to the car, and because most men know this to have happened so many times, they acquiesce.

10.9. Never Giving Up as a Father

The reality, however, is that these are threats that are meant to disempower the father. As a father, you must never give up. From the time you know of the pregnancy, assert your rights. The mother must know that even if you are unmarried, you intend to exercise and discharge your fifty percent share of your obligations.

Once you sense hostility, make sure to have a third party in all your meetings, as this is the time she will fabricate stories of violence against you to try and get a restraining order. You can approach the court and make an application to confirm you as the father.

In case you are accused of being a father, but there is reasonable doubt on your side about this, it is well within your rights to get a paternity test. Because of the risks involved in any medical procedures, I would advise this is done after the child is born, but until then, if there is a chance you are the father, start the parenting plan negotiations with the mother.

10.10. The Importance of a DNA Test

The fear of discovering that a child I've invested in isn't biologically mine is profound, making DNA testing crucial if there's any doubt. Ironically, the stigma surrounding children born out of wedlock has granted unmarried fathers a unique power: the freedom to question paternity without the same constraints as married couples.

In a traditional marriage, questioning paternity can irrevocably damage trust and the relationship itself. But as an unmarried father, my primary concern is my son's well-being, not maintaining a romantic relationship with his mother. This allows me to openly address concerns that might be taboo within a marriage. I'm not seeking approval or affection from her, so there's no need to tiptoe around sensitive topics if they impact my role as a father.

Had we been married, questioning paternity would have jeopardised our entire relationship. Instead, having my son outside of marriage provided the opportunity to confirm his paternity without those complications. This reassurance allows me to dedicate myself fully to him, knowing he truly is a part of me. The peace of mind gained from this knowledge is invaluable, far outweighing any societal judgement about his birth circumstances.

10.11. Defending Against Restraining Orders

If it happens that she applies for a restraining order against you, make sure to go to court and defend it. More often than not, you don't even need to have a lawyer for this, but the important thing is that you must have your facts and evidence in order. From the beginning, when you hear of the pregnancy, confine as much of your conversations to writing for records and future reference. If you ever need to go to court, this is your saving grace. Having a third party come whenever you meet with your child's mother comes in handy to avoid her having an opportunity to fabricate lies against you.

10.12. The Importance of Not Yielding

All these tactics are meant to intimidate you, but whatever happens, do not yield because they are counting on it. A substantial proportion of men who have knowledge of the biassed children's court system give up when they encounter resistance with the mother.

This, however, is a horrible idea because it creates a gap between the father and the child and serves as ammunition for the mother to use later on as proof that you are not involved with the child. Later on, even when you want to get involved with the child, you must first build the relationship from scratch, and the child will not know you.

10.13. The Importance of Family Bonds

It is crucial for the child to know not only you but his extended family as well. If ever something happened to both you and your child's mother, chances are the child will end up with a family member. It is a much better adjustment process when the child is already familiar with the family members that care for them in case of misfortune. There are fewer adjustments for both the child and the family taking them in because they both know each other.

11. Navigating the Children's Courts: A Step-by-Step Guide

After exhausting efforts to resolve issues through amicable discussions and family interventions, you may find yourself needing to approach the courts. The prospect of legal proceedings can understandably feel intimidating, but it's crucial not to be deterred. The Children's Court process is designed to be accessible to families, regardless of financial barriers.

You have the option to represent yourself, and the presiding officer's active role may assist in probing questions that a legal representative would typically handle. Maintain a calm and composed demeanour, objectively present your case, and resist the temptation to allow emotions to overtake rational argument. Remember, the focal point should be the best interests of your child, not personal grievances.

Children's Courts in South Africa share some procedural similarities with other courts, such as adhering to principles of justice and allowing legal representation. However, they differ significantly in their approach and atmosphere:

- These courts are closed to the public, aiming to protect the privacy and confidentiality of minors involved.

- The presiding officer in a Children's Court takes a more interventionist role, actively guiding the proceedings to ensure the child's best interests remain the primary focus.

- The process is designed to be more straightforward, enabling individuals who are self-representing to navigate the system with greater ease.

While the road ahead may seem daunting, a well-prepared and level-headed approach can increase your chances of a favourable outcome. The following step-by-step guide outlines the process, from the initial stages of gathering information to the final court hearing. Ideally, preparation should begin long before you meet the person with whom you will have a child. Once you have met this person, discuss your hopes and expectations, aiming to reach an agreement prior to conception – an agreement you both intend to uphold. However, if such an understanding proves elusive, as is often the case, you can follow this step-by-step guide from the moment you become aware of the pregnancy.

11.1. Gather Information and Documentation

The trigger for this step is you knowing of the pregnancy that you think you are responsible for. Once you know, you approach the mother if she was not the source of the information, and you investigate. It is much better to be sure you are not the father than to suspect you are and do nothing about it.

At best, if the mother tells you that you are not the father and reasonably you think you are not, later on, if it happens that you are, then she can never say you neglected being involved. This should also act as evidence against any retrospective claims of maintenance because you did not know.

In fact, this could be the ground for you as the father to have legal recourse against the mother should it transpire later on that you are the father and she told you that you were not. Her actions would mean she lied and in the process denied you and the child of a relationship with each other.

Collect Documents: Start gathering relevant documents, including your child's birth certificate (proof of paternity), proof of residence, and any evidence of your relationship with the child (photos, emails, witness statements).

11.2. Attempt to Reach an Agreement.

Open communication with the child's mother is crucial. Discuss parenting arrangements (residence, decision-making, and access) and try to reach an amicable agreement. Consider mediation facilitated by a third party to find common ground and create a parenting plan. Where available, your parents are the first stop because, if not for any reason, you as their children are proof of their competence in the subject. Unlike a neutral third party, your parents also have a genetic stake in the child, which makes them likely to consider the long-term consequences of their advice.

11.3. Apply to the Children's Court (If Agreement Fails).

If attempts to reach an agreement fail, you can initiate legal proceedings. This section outlines the steps involved in applying to the Children's Court. It covers the required forms (application and affidavit), how to complete them with details about the child, your desired rights, and supporting evidence. We'll also discuss submitting the application, serving the other party, and the different methods available (personal service, registered mail, sheriff, etc.). Remember, fairness is paramount, both in court and for your child's future perception of the situation.

11.3.1. Required Forms:

○ **Form 2:** Application for Guardianship or Custody of a Child: This form outlines your request for parental rights and responsibilities. You can find it online or obtain it from the court.

○ **Affidavit:** Prepare a sworn statement detailing your circumstances, your relationship with the child, and why you believe you deserve full parental rights and responsibilities.

11.3.2. Populating the Forms:

○ **Form 2:** Fill out all sections accurately, including the child's details, mother's details, and the specific rights and responsibilities you seek (e.g., decision-making, residence, contact time). Briefly explain why these are in the child's best interests.

○ **Affidavit:** Explain your situation in detail. Briefly describe your attempts to reach an agreement with the mother. Highlight your contributions to the child's life (emotional, financial, etc.) and your future plans for their well-being.

○ **Additional Information:** Attach copies of all supporting documents (birth certificate, proof of residence, evidence of relationship with the child).

○ Pay the required court filing fee which is Zero.

11.3.3. Submitting the Application: Visit your local Children's Court and submit the completed Form 2, affidavit, and supporting documents to the court clerk. The court will schedule a hearing date and notify both parties.

11.3.4. Serving the other party: Once the court date is scheduled, the Clerk provides you with the necessary court documents to serve to the other party. This step is essential for ensuring due process, fairness, and the right to be heard.

As a parent, it's essential to be fair to the mother—even during disagreements—ensuring your actions are beyond reproach. Remember, more critical than the court proceedings is the fact that one day your child will review these documents to assess how fairly you handled the situation.

Proper service of court documents like summons, notices of motion, subpoenas, and affidavits is crucial. These can be served personally, by registered mail, through a sheriff, or electronically in some cases. The sheriff's service has a cost but you can utilise the SAPS for free. SAPS members will accompany you to serve the documents, sign them and provide you with the proof of service.

Any disputes over the propriety of service may require additional evidence to confirm that the process was executed correctly.

11.4. The Court Hearing & Decision.

The court hearing is a crucial phase where both parties present their cases regarding the child's best interests. This step triggers the involvement of the Family Advocate, and you will go from the court to the Family Advocate and back to the court again. The process can be broken down into multiple stages:

11.4.1. Initial Court Hearing:

● Both parties appear before the court and present their initial arguments.

● The court assesses the complexity of the case and determines the need for further investigation.

● The court issues a judgement (2 days turnaround time in my experience).

● If deemed necessary, the court will refer the matter to the Family Advocate for an inquiry and report.

11.4.2. Family Advocate Inquiry:

● The Family Advocate conducts an in-depth inquiry into the family situation and the child's best interests.

● This may involve interviews with both parties, the child (if age-appropriate), and other relevant individuals such as family members, teachers, or healthcare professionals.

- The Family Advocate may also request additional documentation or evidence from the parties.

- Based on the inquiry, the Family Advocate prepares a comprehensive report with recommendations for the court.

- It is important to note the glaring discrepancy in how the law is applied to fathers compared to mothers. This inquiry is conducted as a prerequisite for granting a father custody, but the same process is not required when granting a mother automatic custody or in the worst-case scenario where the mother has been incapacitated and the child has to go to the father. This blatant discrimination imposes additional obligations on fathers that are not expected of mothers, highlighting the inherent bias in the system.

11.4.3. Return to Court:

- After receiving the Family Advocate's report, the matter returns to court for further proceedings.

- The court considers the Family Advocate's recommendations along with any additional evidence or arguments presented by the parties.

- The court may hold additional hearings or request further information if necessary.

11.4.4. Throughout this process, it is essential to effectively represent yourself and articulate your case. Here are some key points to keep in mind:

- Prepare a clear and concise argument focusing on the child's best interests.

- Gather relevant evidence, such as witness statements, photographs, or medical reports, to support your case.

- Be ready to respond to the mother's arguments and counter any allegations or concerns raised.

- Maintain a calm and respectful demeanour, even if the proceedings become emotionally charged.

- Take notes during the hearings and keep track of important points or questions that arise.

- While it is possible to represent yourself in these proceedings, it is important to consider seeking legal advice, especially if the case is complex or contentious. A skilled legal professional can provide valuable guidance on how to present your case effectively and navigate the legal process.

○ If you decide to seek legal representation, look for an attorney who specialises in family law and has experience in dealing with Children's Court matters. They can assist you in preparing your arguments, gathering evidence, and responding to the mother's case.

○ However, if you choose to represent yourself, make sure to familiarise yourself with the relevant laws, court procedures, and the Family Advocate's role. Utilise available resources, such as legal aid clinics or online guides, to educate yourself on the process.

11.4.5. Remember, ideally and as per the Constitution the court's primary focus is on the child's best interests, and your arguments should always prioritise your child's well-being. Be prepared to articulate how your involvement and the proposed parenting arrangements will benefit your child's physical, emotional, and developmental needs.

11.4.6. By understanding the court hearing process, the involvement of the Family Advocate, and how to effectively present your case, you can navigate this crucial phase with greater confidence and increase your chances of achieving a favourable outcome for you and your child.

11.5. Challenging the Outcome: Options and Considerations

The South African Constitution and legal system provide multiple avenues for challenging the decisions of various entities, including the courts. While an appeal to a higher court is the most obvious option, there are several other options available to you that often have lower barriers to entry. Understanding these options is crucial in developing a comprehensive strategy to fight for your parental rights and the best interests of your child.

Before considering an appeal, it is essential to explore the various alternatives that can help you challenge the Children's Court's decision. These options include:

11.5.1. Review of Judicial Conduct

If you believe that the magistrate or judge involved in your case has acted unethically or displayed bias, you can file a complaint with the Judicial Service Commission (JSC). The JSC is responsible for investigating allegations of misconduct against judicial officers and taking appropriate disciplinary action when necessary.

11.5.2. Complaint to the Department of Social Development

If you have concerns about the conduct of social workers or other officials involved in your case, you can lodge a complaint with the Department of Social Development. The department has a complaints mechanism in place to address grievances related to the services provided by its staff members.

11.5.3. Engaging with the Family Advocate

If you disagree with the recommendations made by the Family Advocate, you can request a meeting to discuss your concerns and provide additional information or evidence that may influence their report. Building a constructive dialogue with the Family Advocate can help in presenting a more comprehensive picture of your situation.

11.5.4. Mediation or Alternative Dispute Resolution

In some cases, engaging in mediation or alternative dispute resolution processes can help resolve conflicts and reach a mutually agreeable solution without the need for further legal action. This approach can be particularly beneficial in reducing the emotional toll on all parties involved, including the child.

11.5.5. Approaching the Office of the Public Protector:

If you believe that the Children's Court or any other public entity involved in your case has acted improperly or violated your constitutional rights, you can approach the Office of the Public Protector. The Public Protector has the authority to investigate complaints of maladministration, abuse of power, and improper conduct in state affairs.

For a more detailed discussion on the various entities and their roles in challenging decisions related to parental rights, please refer to the chapter on "Multi-pronged strategy and the entities involved." This chapter provides a comprehensive overview of the different organisations and institutions that can be leveraged in your fight for justice.

It is important to remember that challenging the Children's Court's decision is not just a legal battle; it is a war that requires the utilisation of all the resources and skills you have accumulated throughout your life. By adopting a multi-pronged approach and engaging with the various entities available, you can increase your chances of success and ensure that your voice is heard.

Challenging the Children's Court's decision is a difficult and emotionally taxing journey, but it is a fight worth undertaking for the sake of your child. By understanding the various options available to you and developing a comprehensive strategy, you can increase your chances of achieving a favourable outcome and ensuring that your parental rights are upheld.

You can always quit, but remember your son will have to do what you should have done, most likely with less resilience than you have!

You are not alone in this battle. Many fathers have faced similar challenges and have successfully navigated the legal system to secure their rightful place in their children's lives. Draw strength from their experiences and the knowledge that you are fighting for a just and noble cause. On the bright side, once we win this war equality will be the norm, and we can focus our energy into raising our children, rather than fighting an unjust system!

12. Dismantling the Maternal Preference Bias: Upholding Children's Rights and Paternal Bonds

Losing a parent is profoundly traumatic for a child, particularly during their formative years when dependence on consistent caregiving is crucial. The grief of losing a parent is immense and can be exacerbated if the child must also adapt to new environments and caregivers. This adjustment is particularly stark in cases where children, born to unmarried parents, are distant from their fathers due to the ongoing application of the maternal preference rule.

Driven away by legal and societal biases that favour mothers, many fathers diminish their efforts to establish a meaningful bond with their child. Should the mother pass away, the child then faces the additional challenge of building a relationship with a scarcely known father, intensifying the emotional and psychological impact of their loss. This scenario underscores the flawed justifications used to uphold the maternal preference rule.

12.1. Debunking the Breastfeeding Myth

A common justification for maternal preference, particularly during a child's infancy, is the necessity of breastfeeding. However, this argument does not hold up under scrutiny. In reality, many mothers, especially those with careers, return to work within three months of giving birth. During their absence, they express and store breast milk, ensuring that their child is adequately fed by whoever is caring for them.

Ironically, many women are comfortable leaving their child with a relative, nanny, or daycare provider - often someone they've only recently met - for extended periods. Yet, when a father asserts his right to equal participation in childcare, he is often met with the excuse that the child needs their mother. This begs the question: what about the hours when the mother is at work, and the child is under the care of someone else?

12.1.1. Fathers' Capabilities and Modern Parenting

This argument also overlooks the capabilities of fathers, who have demonstrated their ability to fully care for their newborns in tragic circumstances such as the death of the mother during or shortly after childbirth. Such situations clearly refute the notion that fathers are inherently less capable of providing adequate early childcare.

Moreover, the belief that breastfeeding necessitates exclusive maternal care ignores the realities of modern parenting. Expressing and storing breast milk allows mothers to return to work shortly after childbirth while still ensuring their child receives the benefits of breastfeeding. If infants can be entrusted to other caregivers during this stage, fathers should be considered equally capable. This is especially important in preventing the potential trauma of separating a child from their surviving parent in the event of maternal loss.

12.1.2. The Role of Extended Family

Another important factor often overlooked is that fathers, like mothers, have extended families. Just as many women are comfortable leaving their child in the care of their maternal grandmother while they work, the same applies to men. A substantial proportion of men also have sisters with children of their own.

Even if there were any truth to the notion that fathers lack maternal skills for equal parenting (which there is not), this would be compensated for by the involvement of their mothers and sisters. Unlike nannies and preschool employees, paternal grandmothers and aunts have a genetic stake in the child's well-being and a vested interest in ensuring the child receives the best possible care for their long-term development.

12.2. Excuses Cited by Mothers and the Courts

Despite these realities, both mothers and courts continue to use various excuses to uphold maternal preference. Claims that mothers are inherently better nurturers or that young children bond more strongly with their mothers often go unchallenged. Courts, influenced by outdated societal biases and gender norms, frequently favour mothers in custody disputes, undermining the rights of fathers and neglecting the best interests of the child, which should be the primary consideration.

In international contexts, similar biases are observed. In the United States, although the legal system formally recognizes the importance of both parents in a child's life, in practice, courts often exhibit a maternal preference, especially for very young children. This is slowly changing with the increasing recognition of shared parenting and the psychological benefits of involved fatherhood, as supported by research from organisations like the American Psychological Association.

12.3. Constitutional and Legal Consequences

The persistence of the maternal preference rule and the denial of equal paternal rights breach the equality clause of the South African Constitution. Section 9 of the Bill of Rights, emphasising non-discrimination based on sex, alongside rulings from the Constitutional Court, affirms that applying maternal preference in custody disputes is unconstitutional.

Moreover, denying a child access to their parent constitutes not only a violation of the child's best interests but is also actionable under South African law, with potential criminal sanctions outlined in the Children's Act and the Promotion of Equality and Prevention of Unfair Discrimination Act.

12.4. Prioritising the Child's Well-being and Upholding Paternal Bonds

It is crucial for the emotional stability and well-being of a child who has lost a parent to maintain strong bonds with the surviving parent, irrespective of their gender. By fostering relationships between children and both parents, society can offer a semblance of stability and continuity in challenging times. Moving beyond outdated biases to prioritise the well-being and emotional security of children necessitates recognizing the significance of both paternal and maternal bonds.

Denying children the opportunity to establish meaningful relationships with their fathers based on outdated justifications and societal biases is not only unconstitutional but also harmful to their development and overall well-being. It is imperative to dismantle the maternal preference bias and uphold the rights of both parents, ensuring that the best interests of the child remain paramount in all familial and legal decisions.

12.5. The Importance of Familial Bonds

Furthermore, in the tragic event that both parents die, the child will most likely be cared for by a family member - grandparents, uncles, aunts. This underscores the importance of the child being equally familiar with both their maternal and paternal families from the outset. Shared parenting ensures that the child forms strong bonds with both sides of their family, providing a crucial sense of stability and support in the face of such devastating loss.

The perpetuation of the maternal preference bias represents a glaring injustice that undermines the fundamental rights of fathers and children alike. By clinging to outdated stereotypes and flawed justifications, society continues to deprive children of the invaluable opportunity to form strong, nurturing bonds with both parents. This bias not only violates constitutional principles of equality but also disregards a wealth of evidence demonstrating the profound benefits of involved fatherhood for a child's emotional, psychological, and cognitive development.

Denying children access to their fathers based on the unfounded notion that mothers are inherently superior caregivers is not only discriminatory but also detrimental to the well-being of the child. It robs children of the stability, love, and guidance that both parents can provide, especially during the most formative and vulnerable stages of their lives. This bias also fails to acknowledge the realities of modern parenting, where fathers have proven themselves fully capable of providing excellent care, even from infancy.

Moreover, the continued application of the maternal preference rule poses significant risks in the event of maternal loss. By creating distance between fathers and their children, society increases the likelihood of compounding the trauma experienced by these children, forcing them to adapt to unfamiliar environments and caregivers at a time when they need stability and familiarity the most.

It is imperative that society moves beyond these harmful biases and embraces a more equitable and child-centric approach to parenting. This requires a fundamental shift in attitudes, as well as a commitment to upholding the constitutional principles of equality and non-discrimination. Families, communities, and legal systems must work together to dismantle the maternal preference bias and promote the active involvement of both parents in a child's life, regardless of marital status or societal norms.

Only by recognizing the equal importance of maternal and paternal bonds can society truly prioritise the best interests of children. It is through this fundamental shift that children can thrive, benefiting from the love, guidance, and stability provided by both parents, and fostering resilience in the face of life's inevitable challenges.

13. Legal Representation and Self-Advocacy in Children's Matters

In South Africa, the children's court system is intended to be accessible and navigable without the necessity of legal representation. However, the reality often falls short of this ideal, particularly in cases involving child custody and the application of the maternal preference rule. This chapter will explore the challenges and biases within the children's court system, the questionable conduct of some legal representatives, and the potential benefits of self-advocacy in these matters.

13.1. The Illusion of Simplified Proceedings

13.1.1. Children's courts in South Africa claim to offer a simplified process that does not require legal representation.

13.1.2. The intended accessibility aims to ensure that all parties, regardless of their financial means or legal knowledge, can participate in proceedings affecting their children.

13.1.3. However, the complexity of legal procedures, the emotional nature of family disputes, and the inherent biases within the system often make self-representation a daunting task.

13.2. The Persistent Application of the Maternal Preference Rule

13.2.1. Despite legislative changes and the constitutional mandate for gender equality, children's courts in South Africa continue to apply the maternal preference rule in custody cases.

13.2.2. This outdated doctrine presumes that mothers are inherently better suited to be primary caregivers, placing an unfair burden on fathers to prove their competence as parents.

13.2.3. The persistent application of this rule perpetuates gender stereotypes, undermines the principle of the best interests of the child, and denies fathers equal rights and opportunities in their children's lives.

13.3. The Profit-Driven Conduct of Legal Representatives

13.3.1. Legal representatives in child custody cases are bound by their professional code of ethics to prioritise the best interests of the child.

13.3.2. However, some lawyers have been known to exploit the biases within the children's court system for their own financial gain.

13.3.3. Recognizing the courts' tendency to favour mothers, these lawyers may encourage their female clients to seek sole custody and even resort to unethical tactics, such as filing false restraining orders against fathers.

13.3.4. This profit-driven approach not only perpetuates gender inequality but also exacerbates conflict between parents, ultimately harming the well-being of the children involved.

13.4. The Stigma Against Self-Representation

13.4.1. There is a pervasive stigma against self-representation in legal matters, including child custody cases.

13.4.2. This stigma stems from the perception that legal professionals are better equipped to navigate the complexities of the law and argue cases effectively.

13.4.3. However, self-represented litigants often have a deeper understanding of their own circumstances, a stronger emotional investment in the outcome, and a greater willingness to invest time and effort into their cases.

13.4.4. The stigma against self-representation can discourage parents from advocating for their rights and the best interests of their children, perpetuating the reliance on potentially biased legal representatives.

13.5. Empowering Parents Through Legal Education

13.5.1. To facilitate effective self-advocacy, there is a need for greater legal education and resources for parents involved in children's court proceedings.

13.5.2. Community-based organisations, legal aid clinics, and online platforms can provide accessible information on legal rights, court procedures, and strategies for presenting compelling cases.

13.5.3. By empowering parents with the knowledge and tools to advocate for themselves and their children, we can challenge the biases within the system and promote more equitable outcomes.

13.6. The Benefits of Self-Advocacy and Support from Fathers 4 Justice South Africa

Self-advocacy in children's court proceedings can offer several advantages over relying solely on legal representation. Self-represented parents have a direct stake in the outcome of their cases and are motivated to present the strongest possible arguments in favour of their children's well-being. They can provide firsthand accounts of their parenting abilities, their relationships with their children, and the unique dynamics of their families. Self-advocacy also allows parents to maintain control over the narrative of their cases, ensuring that their voices are heard and their perspectives are considered.

In addition to self-advocacy, fathers facing challenges in the family law system can benefit from the support and resources provided by organisations like Fathers 4 Justice South Africa (F4J SA). F4J SA is a civil rights group dedicated to helping alienated fathers gain access to their children and challenging gender-based bias within South Africa's family law system.

F4J SA campaigns for the right of the child to have joint, equal, shared, daily, physical, emotional, psychological contact, care, guardianship, and maintenance with, by, and for both parents at all times. They believe that a child must be able to have a relationship with both biological parents, regardless of the parents' marital status, religious, cultural, or traditional beliefs.

The organisation offers various services to support fathers and families, including:

- Consulting: F4J SA provides consultations to parents in need, offering guidance and support in navigating the family law system and advocating for their parental rights.

- Mediation: They encourage parents to mediate settlements rather than relying on the legal justice system, which often results in a winner and a loser, with the child being the ultimate loser.

- Legal Advice: F4J SA can provide legal advice and support to fathers facing challenges in accessing their children or dealing with false allegations of abuse.

- Advocacy: The organisation advocates for the rights of fathers and children, promoting the importance of joint, equal, shared parenting and challenging systemic biases in the family law system.

Support for Grandparents and Extended Family: F4J SA recognizes the importance of a child's relationship with both maternal and paternal grandparents, aunts, uncles, and cousins, and provides support to ensure that these relationships are maintained.

Domestic Violence Support: F4J SA condemns all forms of violence and offers support to individuals who are being abused or falsely accused of abuse.

By combining self-advocacy with the support and resources provided by organisations like Fathers 4 Justice South Africa, fathers can be better equipped to navigate the challenges of the family law system and work towards achieving the best outcomes for their children. These organisations play a crucial role in empowering fathers, promoting gender equality in parenting, and ensuring that the rights and well-being of children remain at the forefront of family law proceedings.

13.7. Support for Fathers: Organizations and Resources

In addition to Fathers 4 Justice South Africa, several other organisations and resources are dedicated to supporting fathers, families and promoting the best interests of children. These entities provide a range of services, including legal advice, counselling, mediation, and peer support. Some notable organisations and resources include:

- The Family Life Centre:

- Type: Non-profit

- Website: https://familylife.co.za/

- Phone: +27 11 788 7026

- Services: Counseling, mediation, support groups, and workshops for families and individuals facing various challenges.

- Child Welfare South Africa:

- Type: Non-profit

- Website: http://childwelfaresa.org.za/

- Phone: +27 11 482 1414 / 1424 (National Office)

- Email: info@childwelfaresa.org.za

- Services: Child protection, family support, adoption, foster care, and other services focused on the well-being of children.

- Legal Aid South Africa:

- Type: Government

- Website: https://www.legal-aid.co.za/

- Phone: 0800 110 110 (Toll-free)

- Email: Varies by office; contact information for specific offices is available on their website.

- Services: Legal advice and representation for individuals who cannot afford private legal services, including cases related to family law, child custody, and access.

- FAMSA (Families South Africa):

- Type: Non-profit

- Website: https://www.famsaorg.mzansiitsolutions.co.za/

- Phone: +27 11 975 7106/7

- Email: national@famsa.org.za

- Services: Counseling, mediation, parenting skills training, and support for families experiencing challenges, including divorce, separation, and parenting disputes.

- Sonke Gender Justice:

- Type: Non-profit

- Website: https://genderjustice.org.za/

- Phone: +27 11 339 3589

- Email: info@genderjustice.org.za

- Services: Advocacy, education, and community mobilisation to promote gender equality, including engaging men and boys in efforts to end gender-based violence and promote responsible fatherhood.

- Men's Support Groups and Online Forums:

○ Type: Varies; some are civil organisations, others are informal online communities.

○ Website/Contact: Varies depending on the specific group. A simple online search can help you find relevant forums or groups.

○ Services: Peer support, advice, information sharing, and a sense of community for fathers facing similar challenges.

- SAAM (South African Association of Mediators):

○ Type: Professional association

○ Website: https://saam.org.za/

○ Phone: +27 11 447 0467

○ Email: info@saam.org.za

○ Services: Promotes and supports the practice of mediation in South Africa, including family mediation. Can help connect fathers with qualified mediators to resolve parenting disputes.

These organisations and resources offer a wide range of support services for fathers navigating the challenges of the family law system and working to maintain strong, healthy relationships with their children. By leveraging the expertise, guidance, and community support provided by these entities, fathers can be better equipped to advocate for their rights and the well-being of their children.

It is important to note that while these organisations can provide valuable assistance, they should not be viewed as a substitute for legal advice when necessary. Fathers should still consider seeking the guidance of a qualified legal professional, particularly in complex or contentious cases.

Part V: A Father's Fight for Justice

14. My Legal Strategy for Challenging the Children's Court System

As a father who has experienced firsthand the injustices and biases within the children's court system in South Africa, I have decided to take a stand not only for myself and my son and nephews but for all fathers who have been denied their constitutional rights to equality and the best interests of their children. In this chapter, I will detail the legal strategy I am employing to challenge the current system, with the hope that my transparency will empower other fathers to take matters into their own hands and fight for justice.

14.1. Asserting My Rights from Day One

14.1.1. **Communicating with the Mother:** From the moment my son was conceived, I asserted my rights for equality to the mother of my child. Despite her denials, I ensured that she was aware of the constitutional stance, so that she could never claim ignorance of the law.

14.1.2. **Opposing False Allegations:** When the mother of my child, advised by her legal representatives, lied under oath and sought a court order to prevent me from seeing my son on account of alleged violence, I opposed the matter in Criminal court and won. However, the Children's court still confirmed her as the primary parent with all custody, giving me only visiting hours, without providing reasons and contrary to the equality clause and best interests of the child.

14.2. Exhausting Amicable Resolution Attempts

14.2.1. **Giving Time for Resolution:** I provided the mother of my child ample time, over 7 years, to resolve the matter amicably outside of court. She insisted on her approach, which resulted in her having primary custody.

14.2.2. **Approaching the Children's Court:** In February 2024, I approached the children's court for a custody application, seeking full custody. I presented a sworn affidavit alleging criminal behaviour from the mother of my son, alleging reduced capacity as a parent. The court made an order confirming her as the primary parent without supplying reasons for their decision.

14.3. Challenging the Maternal Preference Rule

14.3.1. **Questioning the Court's Bias:** I questioned the court's application of the maternal preference rule and asked them to provide the basis for their decision, which was the mother's replying affidavit. They failed to do so.

14.3.2. **Lodging Complaints:** I lodged the matter with the Commission for Gender Equality and filed a complaint with the Magistrates Commission which escalated into a full ethical complaint against the magistrate regarding their bias.

14.3.3. **Requesting Investigations:** I have requested an investigation from the Law Reform Commission on the conduct of the children's courts, their bias against fathers, and the continued application of the maternal preference rule.

14.4. Taking Legal Action

14.4.1. **Equality Court Application:** I will lodge an application with the Equality Court against the mother for her breach of my constitutional rights. Her actions discriminated against me by denying me equal access to our son. She will be the first respondent, as her actions contravened the equality clause of the constitution and the Equality Act. The children's court will be the second respondent for their bias in affirming the mother's unconstitutional stance.

14.4.2. **Considering Additional Respondents:** I am considering adding my son's mother's legal representatives as the third respondents because all lawyers and attorneys are bound by a code of conduct that requires them to prioritise the best interests of the child in all matters involving children. Their actions were unconstitutional, as they supported the mother in pursuing an unconstitutional stance and colluded with her to fabricate lies against me in court, which they failed to prove.

14.4.3. **Criminal Complaint:** I will lodge a criminal complaint against the mother of my son for endangering his life by employing illegal immigrants as caregivers in her desperation to find childcare.

14.5. Systemic Breach of Constitutional Rights: Grounds for Legal Recourse

Multiple entities within the South African legal system have allegedly violated the constitutional principles of equality before the law and the best interests of the child. This includes:

14.5.1. **The Judiciary:** Courts at all levels have been accused of systematically applying a maternal preference rule, thereby discriminating against fathers and ignoring the best interests of children.

14.5.2. **Private Legal Practitioners:** Some attorneys have reportedly advised or supported mothers in pursuing unconstitutional stances, potentially breaching their professional code of conduct.

14.5.3. **Family Advocates:** These professionals, tasked with representing children's interests, have allegedly failed to protect children from discriminatory rulings and the resulting harm.

14.5.4. **Legislators:** The passage of laws like the Children's Act, containing provisions that may be discriminatory against fathers, has contributed to the systemic violation of constitutional rights.

This list is not exhaustive, as numerous other entities and individuals may have played a role in facilitating or perpetuating this injustice. Any entity that either actively participated in discriminatory actions or had a duty to intervene but failed to do so may be implicated.

The consequences of this systemic discrimination are profound and enduring, affecting multiple generations:

14.5.5. **Fathers:** Unjustly deprived of their rights and relationships with their children, fathers have experienced significant emotional distress and financial burdens.

14.5.6. **Children:** The loss of paternal involvement has been linked to various negative outcomes for children, including increased risk of poverty, behavioural problems, and poor educational attainment.

14.5.7. **Grandparents:** Denied the opportunity to bond with their grandchildren, grandparents have suffered emotional distress and a loss of family connection.

14.5.8. **Extended Families**: The breakdown of family relationships due to discriminatory practices has caused widespread harm and instability.

14.5.9. **Mothers**: Women who were misled into pursuing unconstitutional courses of action may face legal consequences and strained relationships with their children and former partners.

The pursuit of justice for all those affected is not only a matter of individual rights but also a crucial step towards rectifying a systemic injustice and upholding the fundamental principles of the South African Constitution.

14.6. Broader Implications and Societal Change

My legal strategy is not merely a personal battle against the discrimination I have faced as a father; it is a broader challenge to the entire system of state-sanctioned discrimination in South Africa, which operates under the guise of redress and affirmative action. By sharing my approach and the documents I have used to engage with various entities, I aim to inspire and empower not only fathers but all individuals who have been unjustly discriminated against by the state.

Discrimination by the state on the basis of gender, race, or any other immutable characteristic is not only contrary to the principles of equality before the law but also fundamentally incompatible with the best interests of the child. No level of past injustice can justify the implementation of policies that ultimately discriminate against children based on factors beyond their control, compromising their future prospects and well-being.

The youth of South Africa, who were children when the redress provisions of the constitution came into effect, are now bearing the consequences of these state-sanctioned discriminatory policies. The current generation faces unprecedented challenges, including high unemployment rates, escalating violence, poor socio-economic conditions, and other societal ills. These dire circumstances can be directly attributed to affirmative action, employment equity, women empowerment, and other programs that institutionalised discrimination under the pretext of correcting historical wrongs.

It is crucial to recognize that such discriminatory policies, even when implemented with the intention of redress, have had a detrimental impact on the very children they claimed to protect. The bleak reality faced by the youth today serves as a stark reminder that state-sanctioned discrimination, regardless of its purported justification, is never in the best interest of the child.

By openly sharing my story and the tools I have used to challenge the discriminatory practices in the Children's Court system, I hope to contribute to a broader movement against all forms of state-sanctioned discrimination. The templates and documents I have provided, including the complaint to the Magistrates Commission, the submission to the South African Law Reform Commission, and the Equality Court application, can be adapted and utilised by individuals facing various forms of institutionalised discrimination.

As more people join forces to question and challenge the system, our collective voices will grow stronger, pressuring the government to reassess and dismantle policies that perpetuate inequality and injustice. This fight is about creating a society where every individual, regardless of their gender, race, or any other immutable characteristic, is treated equally before the law and where the best interests of children are genuinely prioritised.

Ultimately, by challenging state-sanctioned discrimination and advocating for true equality, we can work towards a future where every child has the opportunity to thrive and reach their full potential, unhindered by the burden of historical injustices or discriminatory policies. Together, we can be the catalyst for change, paving the way for a more just and equitable society for ourselves and future generations.

15. Multi pronged strategy and the entities involved

In the vast landscape of South Africa's legal system, the individual often feels insignificant, a mere speck against the backdrop of powerful institutions like the Children's Court and the High Court. Yet, as Carl Sagan's reflection on the "Pale Blue Dot" reminds us, even the smallest among us holds a place in the universe, and our actions, no matter how seemingly insignificant, can have far-reaching consequences.

This irony is not lost on the countless fathers who have felt marginalized and powerless in the face of a system that seems to favor mothers and disregard their rights. The very institutions they fund through their taxes have become the Goliaths they must confront to secure justice for themselves and their children.

However, South Africa's Constitution, the supreme law of the land, offers a beacon of hope. It empowers every citizen, regardless of their stature, with the same rights and protections, ensuring that even the most powerful entities are subject to the rule of law. This constitutional framework provides a multitude of avenues for redress, including Chapter 9 institutions and legal tools like PAIA and PAJA, which can be wielded by individuals to challenge injustice and demand accountability.

This chapter delves into the multi-pronged strategy employed in this battle for justice, highlighting the various entities and tools that can be leveraged to expose systemic failures, challenge discriminatory practices, and ultimately, ensure that the rights of fathers and the best interests of children are upheld. Remember, in the eyes of the Constitution, we are all equal, and no individual or institution is above the law.

15.1. National Prosecuting Authority (NPA)

The National Prosecuting Authority (NPA) is tasked with instituting criminal proceedings on behalf of the state. Its primary mandate is to ensure that justice is served in cases involving criminal conduct. This involves prosecuting criminal acts and safeguarding the legal process to maintain public trust in the justice system.

The NPA's involvement in my case stems from the criminal elements present, particularly the act of the mother withholding the child without my consent. This act constitutes kidnapping, violating the equality clause of the Constitution and undermining the best interests of the child principle. Addressing these criminal aspects is crucial to ensuring justice is served.

The NPA plays a pivotal role in addressing and prosecuting criminal behaviour related to child custody disputes. Its involvement is essential to uphold the law and ensure that criminal actions, such as the unauthorised withholding of a child, are appropriately prosecuted. By engaging the NPA, I aim to highlight and address the criminal violations that have occurred, thereby safeguarding my child's rights and upholding the principles of justice.

15.2. Commission for Gender Equality (CGE)

The Commission for Gender Equality (CGE) is dedicated to promoting and protecting gender equality in South Africa. It addresses issues of gender discrimination and ensures that the principles of equality before the law are upheld. The CGE plays a critical role in monitoring, investigating, and addressing gender biases and discrimination in various sectors, including the judicial system.

The central issue in my case involves gender discrimination within the judicial system, specifically the application of the maternal preference principle in custody decisions. This bias has significantly impacted the outcome of my case, necessitating the involvement of the CGE to address these unconstitutional practices.

The CGE's mandate to ensure gender equality makes it a vital entity in challenging the biassed practices of the Children's Courts. By involving the CGE, I aim to bring attention to and rectify the gender discrimination that has influenced custody decisions. The CGE's oversight and intervention are crucial in advocating for a fair and just legal process that respects the principles of gender equality and the best interests of the child.

15.3. Magistrates Commission

The Magistrates Commission is responsible for overseeing the conduct of magistrates, ensuring that they uphold the law impartially and justly. It monitors and evaluates the performance of magistrates to maintain the integrity and fairness of the judicial system.

The Magistrates Commission has been approached due to the continued issuance of gender-biassed judgments by magistrates in child custody cases. These judgments are contrary to the law and perpetuate unconstitutional practices that undermine the principles of equality and justice.

By involving the Magistrates Commission, the aim is to hold magistrates accountable for their unconstitutional decisions. Ensuring that magistrates adhere to the principles of equality and the best interests of the child is paramount. The Commission's oversight can lead to reforms and corrective measures that enhance the fairness and impartiality of the judicial process.

15.4. Legal Practice Council (LPC)

The Legal Practice Council regulates the conduct of legal practitioners in South Africa, ensuring adherence to professional standards and ethical practices. It oversees the legal profession to maintain public confidence and uphold the rule of law.

The Legal Practice Council has been approached because private legal practitioners are representing mothers in pursuing unconstitutional stances in custody cases. These practitioners often support and perpetuate gender-biassed approaches, compromising the integrity of the legal process.

The Council's oversight is crucial in addressing professional misconduct by legal practitioners who advocate for gender-biassed and unlawful approaches in child custody matters. By involving the Legal Practice Council, I aim to ensure that legal practitioners uphold ethical standards and support fair, constitutionally compliant practices.

15.5. South African Law Reform Commission (SALRC)

The South African Law Reform Commission (SALRC) investigates and makes recommendations for the reform of South African law. Its goal is to ensure the development and alignment of the law with constitutional principles, addressing gaps and inconsistencies in the legal framework.

The SALRC has been approached to address the broader legal implications of gender bias in child custody cases. By recommending necessary legal reforms, the SALRC can help eliminate discriminatory practices and promote a more equitable legal system.

Engaging with the SALRC is essential for driving systemic changes to eliminate gender discrimination in custody decisions. The Commission's recommendations can lead to legal reforms that align with constitutional principles, ensuring a more just and equitable legal framework for future cases.

15.6. Public Protector South Africa (PP)

The Public Protector is an independent institution established to investigate, report on, and remedy improper conduct in state affairs. It supports and strengthens constitutional democracy by addressing maladministration and ensuring accountability in public offices.

The Public Protector has been approached to investigate the maladministration and improper conduct of the Children's Court in handling my case. Ensuring adherence to constitutional principles and rectifying improper practices are central to the Public Protector's mandate. The Public Protector's oversight can help rectify the improper practices of the court, ensuring that justice is served and the best interests of the child are prioritised. By involving the Public Protector, I aim to address the systemic issues and hold the Children's Court accountable for its actions.

15.7. A Father's Multi-Pronged War for Justice

This chapter provides an overview of the entities involved in the pursuit of justice, their roles, and their relevance to my case. It serves as a guide for understanding the legal avenues available for addressing gender discrimination and ensuring constitutional adherence in child custody matters. The importance of a multifaceted approach in addressing gender bias and ensuring equality cannot be overstated, as these issues touch on both civil and criminal matters.

The involvement of various entities, each with its specific mandate, highlights the complexity and necessity of addressing constitutional violations from multiple angles. From prosecuting criminal behaviour with the NPA to advocating for gender equality with the CGE, holding magistrates accountable with the Magistrates Commission, overseeing legal practitioners with the Legal Practice Council, driving legal reforms with the SALRC, and ensuring accountability with the Public Protector, each entity plays a crucial role.

This chapter serves as a roadmap for fathers and stakeholders navigating the legal landscape to advocate for their rights. It underscores the significance of being tenacious and not being intimidated by any entity or individual, as everyone in South Africa is subject to the same Constitution. By leveraging the resources and mandates of these entities, we can ensure that justice is served, gender discrimination is eradicated, and the best interests of the child are prioritised.

However, the effectiveness of these entities in upholding the Constitution and protecting the rights of fathers and children remains questionable. The persistence of gender bias in child custody cases, despite the constitutional guarantees of equality, raises concerns about the implementation and enforcement of the law. The lack of accountability and transparency within these entities further exacerbates the issue, allowing discriminatory practices to continue unchecked.

Therefore, while the legal framework provides avenues for redress, it is essential to recognize the limitations and potential shortcomings of these entities. Fathers and advocates must remain vigilant and persistent in their pursuit of justice, utilising all available tools and resources to hold these entities accountable and ensure that the principles of equality and the best interests of the child are upheld.

The fight for fathers' rights and gender equality in the family law system is not merely a legal battle; it is a struggle for social justice and the well-being of our children. By understanding the roles and responsibilities of the various entities involved, we can navigate the legal landscape more effectively and work towards a future where all families are treated with fairness, dignity, and respect.

16. The Equality Court Challenge: A Multi-Pronged Strategy for Fathers' Rights

"The murderer rising with the light killeth the poor and needy, And in the night is as a thief. The eye also of the adulterer waiteth for the twilight, Saying, No eye shall see me: And disguiseth his face.".
Job 24:14–15

The fight for fathers' rights and gender equality in the family law system is not just a battle; it is an all-out war against systemic injustice and discrimination. For too long, fathers have been content with small victories, but these have done little to address the deep-rooted biases that plague the children's court and beyond. The consequences of this ongoing injustice are evident in the lives of our children, who are now languishing in a society with the highest unemployment rates, crime levels that rival warzones, rampant gender-based violence, and numerous other social ills.

As fathers, we have been relegated to the status of second-class citizens, deemed suitable only for paying bills and taxes, while watching helplessly as the money we contribute is funnelled into "women empowerment" programs that explicitly exclude boys and men. State-sanctioned discrimination on any grounds, including gender, is fundamentally incompatible with the best interests of the child. The only way to drive this point home is to declare an all-out war on the system that perpetuates these injustices.

In this final chapter before the conclusion, we will delve into the multi-pronged strategy employed in this war, with a particular focus on the pivotal role of the Equality Court. We will examine why the Equality Court application was deliberately pursued as the final step in this process, after engaging with various other entities and compiling their responses and turnaround times. By understanding the strategic importance of this approach, fathers and advocates can effectively leverage the power of the Equality Court to hold these entities accountable, expose systemic injustices, and drive meaningful change.

16.1. Exposing the Darkness: The Limitations of Children's Court Proceedings

16.1.1. The Secrecy and Lack of Transparency

One of the primary reasons why the injustice against fathers has been allowed to thrive is the closed or partially closed nature of children's court proceedings. As the Bible reminds us in Job 24:14-15, "Evil thrives in secret, in darkness." The lack of public scrutiny and accountability in these proceedings has enabled magistrates and court officials to perpetuate discriminatory practices, such as the application of the unconstitutional maternal preference rule, without fear of consequences.

16.1.2. The Unchecked Power of Magistrates

Magistrates in children's courts wield significant influence and have the ability to pick sides in proceedings, a power that is not typically afforded to presiding officers in other courts. This unchecked power has contributed to the systemic bias against fathers, as magistrates often side with mothers and maintain the maternal preference rule, despite its unconstitutionality. The lack of public oversight has allowed this biassed decision-making to go unchallenged, further entrenching the discrimination against fathers in the family law system.

16.2. Unleashing the Power of the Equality Court

16.2.1. Bringing the Battle into the Light

The Equality Court serves as a powerful tool to bring the proceedings of the children's court into public scrutiny. By filing an application with the Equality Court, fathers and advocates can effectively move the discussion and decision-making process from the closed setting of the children's court to an open court. This shift is crucial in exposing the discriminatory practices, holding the court accountable for its actions, and garnering public support for the fight against systemic injustice.

16.2.2. Compelling Accountability from All Fronts

The multi-pronged strategy employed in this war involves first approaching various entities, such as the Commission for Gender Equality, the Magistrates Commission, and the Legal Practice Council, among others. By compiling their responses and turnaround times into a single Equality Court application, fathers and advocates can expose not only the operations of the children's court but also the effectiveness and responsiveness of these entities in upholding the Constitution and protecting the rights of citizens. This approach compels accountability from all fronts, ensuring that no entity can escape scrutiny or responsibility.

16.2.3. Empowering Fathers and Challenging the Status Quo

Many fathers have felt powerless and intimidated when confronted with the biases and discrimination in the family law system. By bringing the operations of these entities into public court through the Equality Court application, fathers and advocates challenge the status quo and empower themselves to assert their rights and demand accountability. This public scrutiny serves as a powerful deterrent against future discriminatory practices and sends a clear message that the time for complacency and small victories is over.

16.3. Leveraging Every Skill and Resource in the War for Justice

16.3.1. A Call to Arms for All Fathers

The war for fathers' rights and gender equality requires the mobilisation of every skill and resource at our disposal. As fathers, we must be willing to bring our best to the fight, leveraging our diverse experiences, knowledge, and networks to mount a formidable challenge against the system that has oppressed us for too long. This multi-pronged strategy is a call to arms for all fathers to stand together, united in our determination to secure justice and equality for ourselves and our children.

16.3.2. Refusing to Settle for Anything Less than Equality

In this war, we refuse to settle for anything less than full equality and the unwavering application of the best interests of the child principle. We will no longer be content with small victories or incremental progress. Either we are treated as equal parents, with the same rights and responsibilities as mothers, or we will continue to fight until justice prevails. The stakes are too high, and the consequences of inaction too severe, for us to accept anything less than a complete overhaul of the discriminatory system.

16.4. Declaring War on All Fronts

16.4.1. Exposing the Complicity of Legal Practitioners

The Equality Court application not only targets the children's court and the entities that have failed to uphold the Constitution but also exposes the complicity of legal practitioners who have exploited the biases in the system for their own gain. By including these legal representatives as respondents in the application, we shine a light on their role in perpetuating the discrimination against fathers and hold them accountable for their actions.

16.4.2. Challenging the High Court's Failure as the Upper Guardian

Ultimately, the responsibility for the ongoing injustice against fathers lies with the High Court, which has failed in its duty as the upper guardian of all children. By virtue of not being a lawyer, I am not beholden to the High Court and can challenge its authority and hold it accountable for its failure to protect the rights of fathers and the best interests of children. This war is not just about individual cases or specific entities but about exposing the systemic failures of the judiciary and demanding reform at the highest levels.

16.5. The Limitations of Children's Court Proceeding.

16.5.1. Closed or Partially Closed Nature of Proceedings

One of the primary reasons why the injustice against fathers has been allowed to thrive is the closed or partially closed nature of children's court proceedings. Unlike open courts, which are subject to public scrutiny and accountability, children's courts operate in a more secretive manner. This lack of transparency has enabled magistrates and other court officials to perpetuate discriminatory practices, such as the application of the unconstitutional maternal preference rule, without fear of public outcry or consequences.

16.5.2. The Unique Role of Magistrates in Children's Courts

Magistrates in children's courts wield significant influence and have the ability to pick sides in proceedings, a power that is not typically afforded to presiding officers in other courts. This unique role has contributed to the systemic bias against fathers, as magistrates often side with mothers and maintain the maternal preference rule, despite its unconstitutionality. The lack of public oversight has allowed this biassed decision-making to go unchecked, further entrenching the discrimination against fathers in the family law system.

16.6. The Strategic Importance of the Equality Court

16.6.1. Bringing Children's Court Proceedings into Public Scrutiny

The Equality Court serves as a powerful tool to bring the proceedings of the children's court into public scrutiny. By filing an application with the Equality Court, fathers and advocates can effectively move the discussion and decision-making process from the closed setting of the children's court to an open court. This shift is crucial in exposing the discriminatory practices, holding the court accountable for its actions, and garnering public support for the fight against systemic injustice.

16.6.2. Compelling Accountability from Various Entities

The multi-pronged strategy employed in this fight involves first approaching various entities, such as the Commission for Gender Equality, the Magistrates Commission, and the Legal Practice Council, among others. By compiling their responses and turnaround times into a single Equality Court application, fathers and advocates can expose not only the operations of the children's court but also the effectiveness and responsiveness of these entities in upholding the Constitution and protecting the rights of citizens. This approach compels accountability from these entities, which are funded by taxpayers' money and have a duty to promote equality and justice.

16.7. Empowering Citizens and Challenging Power Dynamics

Many South Africans feel powerless and intimidated when confronted with authority figures, which has hindered efforts to hold entities accountable for their actions. By bringing the operations of these entities into public court through the Equality Court application, fathers and advocates challenge this power dynamic and empower citizens to assert their rights and demand accountability. This public scrutiny serves as a powerful deterrent against future discriminatory practices and encourages entities to prioritise their constitutional mandates over maintaining the status quo.

16.8. The Role of Legal Professionals and the High Court

16.8.1. The Conflict of Interest in Challenging the Maternal Preference Rule

Legal professionals, both in private practice and within the court system, have been hesitant to challenge the illegality of the maternal preference rule due to the potential consequences they may face from the High Court. As the High Court empowers legal practitioners to practise law, questioning its authority or the status quo could jeopardise their livelihoods. This conflict of interest has led many legal professionals to acquiesce to the injustice and benefit from it, rather than risk their careers by advocating for change.

16.8.2. The Importance of External Advocacy

Given the reluctance of legal professionals to challenge the High Court and the discriminatory practices within the family law system, external advocacy becomes all the more crucial. Fathers, activists, and concerned citizens who operate outside the legal profession have the freedom and means to question the judiciary and the legal system without fear of repercussions to their livelihoods. By advocating for change from the outside, these individuals can apply pressure on the system to reform and hold those in power accountable for their actions.

16.9. Building a Coalition for Change

16.9.1. Uniting Fathers, Activists, and Concerned Citizens

The fight for fathers' rights and gender equality in the family law system is not a solitary endeavour. By uniting fathers, activists, and concerned citizens who share a common vision for justice, we can create a powerful coalition for change. This collective effort amplifies our voices, resources, and impact, ensuring that the discriminatory practices within the children's court and beyond do not go unnoticed or unchallenged.

16.9.2. Leveraging Legal Tools and Strategies

The multi-pronged strategy outlined in this book, culminating in the Equality Court application, provides a comprehensive framework for leveraging legal tools and strategies to combat systemic injustice. By utilising the templates and resources provided, fathers and advocates can effectively navigate the legal landscape, assert their rights, and hold entities accountable for their actions. The collective utilisation of these tools and strategies creates a formidable force for change, one that cannot be easily ignored or dismissed by those in power.

16.10. Conclusion

The multi-pronged strategy employed in the fight for fathers' rights and gender equality, with the Equality Court application as its final and pivotal step, represents a powerful approach to challenging the systemic discrimination within the family law system. By first engaging with various entities and then bringing their responses and the proceedings of the children's court into public scrutiny, fathers and advocates can effectively hold these entities accountable, expose the injustices that have thrived in secrecy, and drive meaningful change.

This strategy recognizes the limitations of the closed nature of children's court proceedings and the unique role of magistrates in perpetuating bias against fathers. It leverages the power of the Equality Court to bring these issues into the public domain, compelling accountability and empowering citizens to assert their rights.

Furthermore, this approach acknowledges the reluctance of legal professionals to challenge the status quo and the importance of external advocacy in applying pressure on the system to reform. By building a coalition of fathers, activists, and concerned citizens, and leveraging legal tools and strategies, we can create a formidable force for change that cannot be easily ignored or dismissed.

As we move forward in this fight, let us draw strength from the knowledge that we are not alone. By uniting our efforts, sharing our experiences, and leveraging the power of the Equality Court and other legal mechanisms, we can work towards dismantling the discriminatory practices that have long plagued the family law system. Together, we can create a society where the rights of fathers and the best interests of children are truly upheld, and where justice and equality prevail.

17. The Case for Open Courts in Children's Proceedings

Section 34 of the South African Constitution enshrines the right to have legal matters heard in an open court. This principle is fundamental to a transparent and accountable judicial system, ensuring that justice is not only done but seen to be done. The Constitution affirms that

"Everyone has the right to have any dispute that can be resolved by the application of law decided in a fair public hearing before a court or, where appropriate, another independent and impartial tribunal or forum."

Open court proceedings allow public scrutiny, fostering trust in the judicial system and ensuring that justice is applied fairly and equitably. This transparency is especially crucial in cases involving constitutional or legal breaches, where public awareness and oversight are key to maintaining accountability and integrity.

17.1. The Best Interests of the Child: A Justification for Closed Proceedings

Children's courts in South Africa often operate with closed or partially closed proceedings, justified under Section 28(2) of the Constitution, as being under the child's best interests. The rationale is that closed proceedings protect the child's privacy and emotional well-being, shielding them from the potentially harmful exposure of open court processes.

However, while this protection is vital when the child's direct involvement is necessary, it does not extend to all issues adjudicated in children's courts. Matters concerning constitutional rights, parental competency, or allegations of criminal conduct by one parent often do not require the child's presence or direct involvement. Despite this, these matters are still heard in closed proceedings, limiting transparency and public scrutiny.

17.2. The Consequences of Closed Proceedings: Injustice Against Fathers

Closed or partially closed proceedings in children's courts have led to significant injustices, particularly against fathers. The lack of transparency has perpetuated gender stereotypes that have been largely eliminated in other areas, such as the workplace and education. This inconsistency is evident in the judicial system's continued bias against fathers in child custody cases.

- **Perpetuation of Gender Stereotypes:** Closed proceedings have allowed outdated stereotypes about paternal roles to persist unchallenged. These stereotypes include assumptions that mothers are inherently more suited to caregiving roles, while fathers are less capable of nurturing and providing emotional support.

- **Lack of Public Accountability:** Without public scrutiny, judicial officers may apply personal biases or outdated norms without fear of external accountability. This has led to decisions that contravene constitutional guarantees of equality and fair treatment, particularly under Section 9 of the Constitution, which provides for equal protection and benefit of the law.

- **Concealment of Judicial Misconduct:** The secrecy of children's courts shields judicial officers from scrutiny regarding their adherence to constitutional principles. This lack of oversight has facilitated decisions that favor maternal preference over paternal rights, undermining the constitutional mandate for equality before the law.

17.3. Deviations in Judicial Roles: The Unnecessary Departure from Standard Practices

Another significant deviation in children's courts is the role of the judicial officer. Unlike in other civil and family law proceedings, judicial officers in children's courts often take on a more inquisitorial role, which can lead to subjective interpretations and applications of the law.

- **Inquisitorial vs. Adversarial Roles:** In children's courts, judicial officers may actively investigate and question parties, blurring the lines between impartial adjudication and advocacy. This inquisitorial approach contrasts with the adversarial system prevalent in other courts, where the judge remains a neutral arbiter while parties present their cases.

- **Impact on Fairness and Objectivity:** This deviation has contributed to inconsistent application of legal standards and principles, particularly regarding paternal rights. The subjective nature of judicial intervention in these cases can lead to decisions that reflect personal biases rather than legal merits.

- **No Justification for Deviation:** The deviation in the judicial role is unnecessary and has contributed to perpetuating constitutional breaches. Other civil and family law proceedings, which deal with sensitive and personal matters, successfully operate with a more neutral and transparent judicial approach. There is no compelling reason why children's courts should not align with these practices, especially given the significant impact on fathers' constitutional rights.

17.4. The Argument for Open Proceedings in Children's Courts

Given the significant impact of closed proceedings on fathers and the perpetuation of gender stereotypes, it is essential to reconsider the necessity of such secrecy in children's courts.

- **Objective Evaluation in Open Court:** Issues such as parental competency, constitutional breaches, and criminal allegations can and should be evaluated objectively in open court. These matters often do not require the child's involvement and can be adjudicated based on evidence and legal principles, much like other family law and civil cases.

- **Consistency with Constitutional Provisions:** Aligning children's courts with the constitutional mandate for open proceedings ensures consistency in the application of justice. Only segments of proceedings that directly involve the child or require their testimony should be closed, while other matters can be transparently adjudicated.

- **Public Scrutiny and Accountability:** Open proceedings allow for public oversight, fostering a judicial environment that is accountable and fair. This transparency helps prevent biases and ensures that judicial officers adhere to constitutional principles.

17.5. Lessons from the Past 30 Years: The Impact of Closed Proceedings

The past three decades of closed or partially closed proceedings have not resulted in better outcomes for the children of South Africa. Instead, the current generation faces high unemployment, increased crime rates, and various social challenges. These outcomes suggest that the secrecy of children's courts has not served the best interests of children as intended.

● **Worse Outcomes for "Born Frees":** The generation born after apartheid, who should have benefited most from democratic reforms, faces significant socio-economic challenges. The lack of transparency in children's courts has contributed to these adverse outcomes by allowing judicial biases to go unchecked, undermining paternal involvement and support.

● **Need for Reform:** To improve outcomes for future generations, it is crucial to reform children's courts to ensure greater transparency and adherence to constitutional principles. Open proceedings, except where directly involving the child, can help achieve a more equitable and accountable judicial system.

17.6. Conclusion: Aligning Children's Courts with Constitutional Values

Reforming children's courts to align more closely with the constitutional provision for open courts is essential for ensuring justice and fairness. By restricting closed proceedings to matters that directly involve the child, the system can uphold the rights of fathers and ensure that all parties receive equal treatment under the law.

The current practices in children's courts have led to significant injustices and have perpetuated gender stereotypes. A shift towards greater transparency and accountability is necessary to correct these issues and ensure that the judicial system serves the best interests of all parties involved, particularly the children it aims to protect.

18. Managing Expectations and Holding Entities Accountable

One of the most disheartening experiences is going through the arduous process of building a case and filing a complaint, only to receive no response or even when they do respond, they show no interest in the case and fail to take any accountability. The truth is, if the entities involved in this process were truly fulfilling their duties and being held accountable, fathers and boys would not still be fighting this battle in 2024, 30 years after the principles of equality before the law and the best interests of the child were enshrined in our Constitution.

18.1. Extent of Neglect Faced by Fathers

To illustrate the extent of neglect faced by fathers, it is important to note that since the Constitution came into effect, not only have legal instruments been implemented to prevent discrimination against women and girls in formal education and the workplace, but affirmative action measures, many of which are discriminatory towards men and boys, have been sanctioned by the state to ensure women are integrated and given a larger share in the formal workplace. However, no such measures have been implemented for men and boys. There are worldwide programs like "Take a Girl to Work" and tax-funded initiatives for women empowerment, but no equivalent programs exist for boys and men. This stark disparity is a clear indictment of the failure of the entities responsible for protecting the best interests of children and ensuring adherence to the Constitution.

18.2. Scepticism Towards Accountability

You might ask yourself, if these entities have failed thus far and have not been held accountable for their failures, why would they start to care now simply because you have raised the issue with them? It is no secret that even I am extremely sceptical of entities like the Commission for Gender Equality (CGE), which should be an example of the principles it claims to stand for, yet has championed discrimination in its own employment practices. In my article "South Africa: A Country where Irony is the Norm," I explored the failures and inconsistencies of the CGE in detail.

The CGE's employee profile does not match the country's race and gender demographics, despite being an institution with oversight powers on gender equality. One would expect such an entity, whose very existence is justified by the need to address inequality, to set an example. However, the CGE has consistently failed to do so throughout its existence. This raises the question of how the CGE can effectively address gender inequality in society when it has not been able to achieve equality within its own ranks.

18.3. Strategies for Accountability

Similarly, the same ineptitude and complacency facilitated by affirmative action policies that lowered standards and neglected merit have allowed incompetent individuals to work in these entities, knowing they can get away with not doing their jobs. Thankfully, the Constitution also provides measures to combat this.

In my case, the first strategy I will employ to bring the workings of these entities to light is through the Equality Court application. All the submissions I make to these entities will be part of my Equality Court application. As court proceedings are open to the public to facilitate accountability, the progress and responses from these entities will now be subject to the same public scrutiny as they should have been in response to my submissions.

18.4. Legal Tools: PAIA and PAJA

My career in compliance has also taught me about the Promotion of Access to Information Act (PAIA) and the Promotion of Administrative Justice Act (PAJA). Both these statutes allow the public to have access to the processes of entities and hold them accountable for their decisions. Do not despair if you feel that the only way to bring an entity to account is through costly legal proceedings. Tools like PAIA and PAJA provide accessible avenues for the layperson with low barriers to entry.

PAIA applies to both public and private institutions, allowing us to scrutinise their processes and policies. It is these policies that we can then audit for compliance. For example, if I submit a complaint to the CGE, according to its processes, the CGE must respond to that complaint in writing within a specified time frame. Should they fail to do so, it constitutes a breach of their own policies, which can be escalated to either the Information Regulator or pursued through the courts.

18.5. Comprehensive Approach to Accountability

Remember, the goal is to approach this issue from all sides, utilising all the skills we have acquired, from risk management to compliance management, auditing to root cause analysis, and so on. Rather than despairing over the failure of government and judiciary employees to perform their duties, we must exploit every legal avenue to hold them accountable. With tools like PAIA and PAJA, we have a strong starting point.

Even private entities, such as legal representatives who intimidate fathers and exploit mothers, are not beyond scrutiny. PAIA applies to both private and public entities, enabling us to examine their practices and hold them accountable for any unethical or discriminatory conduct.

18.6. Additional Tools and Mechanisms for Accountability

In addition to PAIA and PAJA, there are other tools and mechanisms that can be used to hold entities accountable and seek redress:

18.6.1. **The Public Protector (PP):** The PP is an independent institution established by the Constitution to investigate any conduct in state affairs or the public administration that is alleged or suspected to be improper or to result in any impropriety or prejudice. Complaints can be lodged with the Public Protector's office, and they have the power to investigate and take appropriate remedial action.

18.6.2. **The South African Human Rights Commission (SAHRC):** The SAHRC is mandated by the Constitution to promote, protect, and monitor human rights in South Africa. If you believe that your human rights or the rights of your child have been violated by any entity, you can lodge a complaint with the SAHRC, and they will investigate and take appropriate action.

18.6.3. **The Judicial Service Commission (JSC):** The JSC is responsible for the appointment, promotion, and discipline of judges. If you believe that a judge has acted improperly or displayed bias in a case involving parental rights, you can lodge a complaint with the JSC, and they will investigate and take appropriate disciplinary action.

18.6.4. **The Health Professions Council of South Africa (HPCSA):** If you have concerns about the conduct of a healthcare professional involved in a case, such as a psychologist or social worker, you can lodge a complaint with the HPCSA. They have the power to investigate and discipline healthcare professionals who breach their ethical duties.

18.7. Collective Efforts for Change

By utilising these various tools and mechanisms, we can work towards holding entities accountable, exposing their shortcomings, and advocating for change. It is through the collective efforts of fathers, activists, and concerned citizens that we can challenge the systemic biases and discrimination that have long plagued the family law system in South Africa.

As we embark on this journey, let us draw strength from the knowledge that we are not alone in this fight. By sharing our experiences, supporting one another, and leveraging the legal tools at our disposal, we can work towards creating a more just and equitable society for all families. Together, we can hold those in power accountable and pave the way for a brighter future where the rights of fathers and the best interests of children are truly upheld.

Part VI: Conclusion and Additional Resources

19. Conclusion: Goliath's Fall

Throughout this book, we have embarked on a journey that challenges the very foundations of our societal structures and the systems that govern our lives. From the education system to healthcare, from the energy sector to municipal services, we have witnessed the pervasive failures of formal institutions and the credentials they tout as markers of competence. We have seen how these failures disproportionately impact the most vulnerable among us, particularly the black majority in South Africa, who continue to bear the brunt of inadequate service delivery and institutional dysfunction.

My personal experiences, as a homeschooling father and an individual fighting for equal parental rights, have served as a microcosm of the broader struggles we face as a society. By challenging the children's court system and the biases entrenched within it, I have come to understand the importance of individual action in the face of systemic injustice. The lessons I have learned along the way have been invaluable, not only for my own journey but for anyone who wishes to challenge the status quo and reclaim their autonomy.

One of the most crucial lessons has been the power of perseverance. Challenging deeply entrenched norms and institutions can be a daunting task, and the road to change is often riddled with obstacles and setbacks. However, it is through unwavering commitment and resilience that we can hope to make progress. Whether it is fighting for equal parental rights, advocating for alternative education models, or demanding accountability from our public and private institutions, we must remain steadfast in our pursuit of justice.

Another key lesson has been the importance of empowering oneself with knowledge and understanding. To effectively challenge the systems that govern our lives, we must first understand how they operate and identify the ways in which they fall short. This requires a willingness to question the accepted narratives, to seek out alternative perspectives, and to critically examine the evidence before us. By arming ourselves with knowledge, we can more effectively advocate for change and hold those in power accountable.

Throughout this book, we have also seen the transformative potential of individual and collective action. From the residents of Kgetlengrivier taking control of their water and sewerage systems to the community-driven solutions emerging in the face of government failure, we have witnessed the power of people coming together to effect change. As individuals, we may feel powerless against the Goliaths of our society - the entrenched institutions and the credentials that prop them up. However, by joining forces with others who share our struggles and our vision for a more just and equitable society, we can amplify our voices and our impact.

To those who find themselves facing their own Goliaths, whether in the form of a biassed legal system, a failing education model, or a dysfunctional public service, I offer the following guidance: First, know that you are not alone. There are countless others who share your struggles and your desire for change. Seek them out, build alliances, and learn from their experiences. Second, arm yourself with knowledge and understanding. Question the accepted narratives, and seek out alternative perspectives. Third, be prepared for a long and difficult journey. Change rarely comes easily or quickly, but with perseverance and resilience, it is possible. Finally, remember that every individual action, no matter how small, contributes to the larger tide of change. Your voice, your story, and your struggle matter.

As we conclude this book, I want to emphasise that the fall of Goliath is not the end of the story. It is merely the beginning of a new chapter - one in which we, as individuals and as a society, have the opportunity to reimagine and rebuild our institutions and systems in a way that truly serves the needs and aspirations of all people. It is a chapter that calls for a fundamental rethinking of the role of credentials and formal education, and a greater recognition of the value of practical skills, moral integrity, and community-driven solutions.

The journey ahead will not be easy, but it is one that we must undertake if we hope to create a more just and equitable society for ourselves and for future generations. As we embark on this path, let us draw strength from the knowledge that we are part of a larger movement for change, and that every step we take, every battle we fight, brings us closer to the fall of Goliath and the rise of a new era of individual and collective empowerment.

To my son, my nephews, and all those who will come after us, I leave you with this message: The fight for justice and equality is a lifelong struggle, but it is one that is worth every ounce of effort. As you navigate the challenges and obstacles that lie ahead, remember the lessons we have learned and the battles we have fought. Remember that you have the power to challenge the status quo and to shape the world in which you live. And remember that, even in the face of the most towering Goliaths, change is possible when we stand together and fight for what is right.

20. About the Author and Other Works

For those interested in exploring related topics and gaining more insights, I have authored several other books and created audiobooks available for free on my YouTube channel. These resources cover a range of subjects from personal growth to historical exploration and educational strategies.

20.1. Books by Salatiso Lonwabo Mdeni

20.1.1. Getting to Know Yourself as a South African[1]

This book delves into the cultural and historical aspects of self-identity, offering readers a comprehensive understanding of what it means to be South African.

20.1.2. Unravelling Xhosa History[2]

Explore the rich history of the Xhosa people, their traditions, and their significant contributions to South African heritage.

20.1.3. Maximise[3] Your Child's Education with the Homeschooling Father[4]

This guide offers practical advice and strategies for fathers who are considering or currently engaged in homeschooling their children.

20.2. Free Audiobooks & Articles on YouTube

I also have several audiobooks available for free on my YouTube channel. These audiobooks provide accessible and engaging content on various topics.

20.2.1. Getting to Know Yourself as a South African - Audiobook[5]

This audiobook version offers an immersive experience into the cultural identity and self-discovery journey of South Africans.

20.2.2. Unravelling Xhosa History - Audiobook[6]

Listen to the captivating history of the Xhosa people and gain a deeper appreciation for their heritage.

20.2.3. Maximise[7] Your Child's Education with the Homeschooling Father - Audiobook[8]

1. https://www.google.co.za/search?tbo=p&tbm=bks&q=inauthor:%22Salatiso%22

2. https://www.amazon.com/stores/author/B0CSH6PJLP/allbooks?ingress=0&visitId=d9a2c8b4-9226-460c-8cdc-42fc5812ce7e&ref_=ap_rdr

3. https://www.amazon.com/stores/author/B0CSH6PJLP/allbooks?ingress=0&visitId=d9a2c8b4-9226-460c-8cdc-42fc5812ce7e&ref_=ap_rdr

4. https://www.amazon.com/stores/author/B0CSH6PJLP/allbooks?ingress=0&visitId=d9a2c8b4-9226-460c-8cdc-42fc5812ce7e&ref_=ap_rdr

5. https://www.youtube.com/watch?v=xzVtMWJqR4w&list=PLXPU1hLJ2t0PpWsmzaNxfCErwusjoiFNW

6. https://youtube.com/playlist?list=PLXPU1hLJ2t0PpWsmzaNxfCErwusjoiFNW&si=VRl6GUfJm4Cdiu_T

7. https://youtube.com/playlist?list=PLXPU1hLJ2t0PpWsmzaNxfCErwusjoiFNW&si=VRl6GUfJm4Cdiu_T

8. https://youtube.com/playlist?list=PLXPU1hLJ2t0PpWsmzaNxfCErwusjoiFNW&si=VRl6GUfJm4Cdiu_T

This audiobook provides fathers with the knowledge and confidence to take an active role in their children's education through homeschooling.

20.3. Salatiso Lonwabo Mdeni on YouTube

To learn more about the author and his work, you can:

- Visit hisYouTube channel[9], where you can find audiobook versions of his books and other engaging content.

- Explore hisauthor page on Google Books[10], which showcases his published works.

- Check out hisauthor page on Amazon[11], where you can find his books available for purchase.

By engaging with the author's diverse range of works, you can gain a deeper understanding of the issues he is passionate about and the unique perspectives he brings to the table. Whether you are a father navigating the complexities of the family law system, a parent exploring alternative education options, or someone eager to learn more about South African history and culture, Salatiso's books and audiobooks offer valuable insights and inspiration.

---

9. https://www.youtube.com/channel/UC2vTLXNNGEr06_HmhRMd7Pw

10. https://www.google.co.za/search?tbo=p&tbm=bks&q=inauthor:%22Salatiso%22

11. https://www.amazon.com/stores/author/B0CSH6PJLP/allbooks?ingress=0&visitId=d9a2c8b4-9226-460c-8cdc-42fc5812ce7e&ref_=ap_rdr

Appendices

References

1. Legal Documents and Legislation
    1. South African Constitution, 1996. Available at: https://www.gov.za/documents/constitution-republic-south-africa-1996
    2. Children's Act 38 of 2005. Available at: https://www.gov.za/documents/childrens-act
    3. Promotion of Access to Information Act 2 of 2000 (PAIA). Available at: https://www.justice.gov.za/legislation/acts/2000-002.pdf
    4. Promotion of Administrative Justice Act 3 of 2000 (PAJA). Available at: https://www.justice.gov.za/legislation/acts/2000-003.pdf
    5. Equal Status and Human Rights Law. Available at: https://www.gov.za/documents/constitution/chapter-2-bill-rights
    6. Legal Practice Act 28 of 2014. Available at: https://www.lpc.org.za/

1. Books and Articles
    1. Moyo, Khanyisile. Gender and the Judiciary in Africa: From Obscurity to Parity? Routledge, 2018.
    2. Du Toit, Francois. Legal Framework for Family Law in South Africa. Juta and Company Ltd, 2013.
    3. Lamb, Michael E.The Role of the Father in Child Development. Wiley, 2010.
    4. Montgomery, Heather. Childhood and Society: Growing Up in an Age of Uncertainty. Polity, 2014.
    5. Eekelaar, John, and Roberts, Simon. Family Law and Social Policy. Butterworths, 1984.
    6. Glennon, Theresa. Gender and Parenting: The Role of Law and Legal Systems. Elgar Publishing, 2019.
    7. Levit, Nancy. The Gender Line: Men, Women, and the Law. New York University Press, 1998.
    8. Goldstein, Joseph, et al. Beyond the Best Interests of the Child, Free Press, 1973.

1. Reports and Guidelines
    1. UNICEF. The Best Interests of the Child in South African Family Law: A Report on Child Custody, Access and Maintenance. 2010. Available at: https://www.unicef.org/southafrica/reports/best-interests-child-south-africa
    2. South African Law Reform Commission. Discussion Paper 105: Review of the Law of Evidence and the Conduct of Trials in Civil and Criminal Cases. 2004. Available at: http://salawreform.justice.gov.za/dpapers/dp105.pdf. Commission for Gender Equality (CGE). Report on Gender Representation and Participation in South Africa. 2021. Available at: https://www.cge.org.za/
    3. National Prosecuting Authority (NPA). Annual Report 2023/2024. Available at: https://www.npa.gov.za/
    4. Public Protector South Africa. Annual Report 2023/2024. Available at: https://www.pprotect.org/

1. Historical and Cultural References
    1. Mandela, Nelson. Long Walk to Freedom: The Autobiography of Nelson Mandela. Little, Brown and Company, 1994.
    2. Biko, Steve. I Write What I Like: Selected Writings. Picador Africa, 2004.
    3. Mgidlana, Dumisani. Ubuntu: African Management Philosophy. Knowres Publishing, 2006.

4. Du Bois, W.E.B. The Souls of Black Folk. Penguin Classics, 1996.

1. Digital and Online Resources
    1. Fathers 4 Justice South Africa. Support and Advocacy for Fathers in South Africa. Available at: https://www.fathers4justice.org.za/
    2. YouTube Channel - Salatiso Lonwabo Mdeni. Available at: https://www.youtube.com/channel/SalatisoLonwaboMdeni
    3. South African Legal Information Institute (SAFLII). Available at: http://www.saflii.org/

1. Relevant Theories and Concepts
    1. Sagan, Carl. Pale Blue Dot: A Vision of the Human Future in Space. Random House, 1994.
    2. Odysseus' Quotes and Greek Mythology. Homer's Odyssey translated by Robert Fagles. Penguin Books, 1996.
    3. Smith, Adam. The Wealth of Nations. Bantam Classics, 2003.
    4. Locke, John. Two Treatises of Government. Yale University Press, 2003.

GOLIATH'S RECKONING: UNVEILING THE BIASSED TRUTH BEHIND CHILDREN'S COURT THAT DISCRIMINATES AGAINST FATHERS

Putting the Law into Action: Templates and Resources for Fathers

Knowing what you need to do is one thing, but putting it into action is another. One of the most significant challenges I faced from the outset was writing a simple affidavit. While articulating the words themselves wasn't the issue, the overwhelming emotion and anger I felt at having to resort to the courts to demand what is constitutionally mine made the process difficult. These feelings didn't subside as the proceedings progressed or as I approached various entities for assistance. To navigate these challenges, I had to develop documents and templates to effectively communicate with these organisations.

I believe that many fathers face similar struggles, which is why I have dedicated this chapter to providing templates that can be used when approaching different entities, including the children's court, the family advocate, the Commission for Gender Equality, the Magistrates Commission, the Legal Practice Council, the National Prosecuting Authority, the Law Reform Commission, and the Public Protector, among others. These templates are designed to guide you through the process of compiling affidavits and submissions.

It's important to note that while the templates provided in this chapter serve as a starting point, it's essential to seek the most up-to-date forms and information directly from the relevant courts and entities. The purpose of these templates is to assist with the content and structure of your documents, but for the most current forms, please visit the following:

1. Children's Court Forms (as per the Children's Act 38 of 2005):

a. Form 2 - Bringing a matter to the children's court (J767 (justice.gov.za)[1])

b. Other forms can be found on the DoJCD website Justice/Forms/Child Justice & Children's Act[2] https://www.justice.gov.za/forms/form_cj.html

2. Family Advocate Forms and details can be found on Justice/Family Advocate/Home[3] (https://www.justice.gov.za/FMAdv/f_main.htm)

3. Equality Court Forms (as per the Promotion of Equality and Prevention of Unfair Discrimination Act 4 of 2000):

a. Form 2 [J693] in 11 languages are available, the English version (https://www.justice.gov.za/EQCact/forms/eqc_form2_J693.pdf)

In addition to the forms and templates, there are various entities and support groups available to help fathers navigate the legal system. These organisations, some of which are covered in this book, can provide invaluable guidance and support throughout the process.

Remember, you are not alone in this journey. Many fathers have faced similar challenges and have successfully advocated for their rights and the well-being of their children. By utilising the templates and resources provided in this chapter, and by seeking support from the various organisations dedicated to assisting fathers, you can effectively put the law into action and work towards a positive outcome for yourself and your children.

---

1. https://www.justice.gov.za/forms/child/ChildrensAct_J767%20%5B20230315%5D.pdf

2. https://www.justice.gov.za/forms/form_cj.html

3. https://www.justice.gov.za/FMAdv/f_main.htm

As you proceed, keep in mind that the emotions you experience are valid and understandable. The legal system can be daunting, and the challenges you face may feel overwhelming at times. However, by arming yourself with knowledge, utilising the available resources, and staying committed to your children's best interests, you can navigate this process with greater confidence and resilience.

Affidavit

IN THE CHILDREN'S COURT FOR THE DISTRICT OF [DISTRICT NAME] HELD AT [COURT LOCATION]

In the matter between:
[Your Full Name], Applicant
and
[Mother's Full Name], Respondent

Case No.: [Case Number]

AFFIDAVIT

I, [Your Full Name], the Applicant in this matter, state under oath:

1. Personal Information:

a. I am the biological father of [Child's Full Name], born on [Date of Birth].

b. I reside at [Your Address].

c. My contact details are [Your Contact Details].

2. Relationship with the Child:

a. [Detail your involvement in the child's life, including care, and emotional connection].

3. Parental Rights and Responsibilities Sought: [Specify the rights you are seeking, e.g., full parental rights and responsibilities, primary residence, specific contact schedule].

4. Reasons for Seeking These Rights: [Explain why granting you these rights is in the child's best interests, citing evidence of your ability to provide a stable and loving environment, your involvement in the child's life, and any concerns about the other parent's care].

5. Attempts at Amicable Resolution: [Describe any attempts you have made to reach an agreement with the mother, including mediation or other forms of negotiation].

6. Supporting Evidence: [Attach any relevant documents, such as the child's birth certificate, proof of residence, photos, communication records, or reports from professionals].

I swear that the contents of this affidavit are true and correct to the best of my knowledge and belief.

[Your Signature, Full Name,Date]
SIGNED AND SWORN TO before me at [Place] on this [Day] day of [Month], [Year].

The Magistrates Commission

Template for a complaint to the Magistrates Commission and the Children's Court regarding the conduct of magistrates in matters involving parental rights and responsibilities:

I, [Your Full Name], hereby lodge a formal complaint against the following magistrates:

1. [Magistrate 1 Name], [Court]
2. [Magistrate 2 Name], [Court]
3. [Add more if applicable]

I am the biological father of [Child/Children's Names and Ages]. The biological mother is [Mother's Full Name].

In proceedings before the above-mentioned magistrates involving the allocation of parental rights and responsibilities, I believe that the magistrates have acted unconstitutionally and unethically by:

1. Applying the maternal preference rule and unfairly discriminating against me as a father, despite the rule being inconsistent with the equality provisions in the Constitution, the Children's Act and the Promotion of Equality and Prevention of Unfair Discrimination Act. The Constitutional Court in President of the Republic of South Africa v Hugo affirmed that there is no rule of law favouring mothers over fathers.
2. Failing to uphold their duty under the Constitution and their oath of office to apply the law impartially and without fear, favour or prejudice. Equality before the law requires that both parents have equal rights and responsibilities from the birth of their child, and the burden of proof is on the party seeking to deprive a parent of those rights.
3. Issuing orders that unjustly deprive me of my parental rights and responsibilities, effectively facilitating the mother's unlawful withholding of the child from me. This may amount to parental child abduction or kidnapping under South African criminal law. By enabling such conduct, the magistrates may be exposing themselves to potential liability as accomplices to these crimes.
4. Breaching the ethical duties in the Code of Conduct for Magistrates to uphold the Constitution, maintain independence and impartiality, and act honourably and in a manner befitting judicial office. Knowingly violating parents' constitutional rights and issuing discriminatory orders brings the magistracy into disrepute.

In light of these serious allegations of unconstitutional, unlawful and unethical conduct, I request that the Magistrates Commission and Children's Court investigate this complaint thoroughly. If the magistrates are found to have violated their constitutional and ethical duties, I urge the Commission and Court to take appropriate disciplinary action, including but not limited to:

- Recommending to the Minister that the magistrates be removed from office under section 13 of the Magistrates Act;

- Ordering the magistrates to undergo additional training on parental rights, children's best interests and constitutional non-discrimination;

- Overturning orders that unfairly discriminate against fathers and reformulating parenting arrangements in line with the constitutional principle of parental equality.

The conduct of these magistrates not only prejudices my individual rights as a father, but undermines public confidence in the impartiality and integrity of the magistracy as a whole. Swift and decisive action is needed to uphold the Constitution, protect children's best interests, and ensure that all parents, regardless of gender, are treated equally before the law.

I am willing to cooperate fully with any investigation and provide further information as required.

Sincerely,

[Your Name]

Legal Practice Council (LPC)

Complaint to the Legal Practice Council (LPC) against legal practitioners and their firms based on the grounds that they facilitated or endorsed the unlawful deprivation of a father's parental rights and responsibilities, potentially amounting to accomplice liability for parental child abduction or kidnapping under South African criminal law.

To: The Legal Practice Council
[Address]
From: [Your Full Name]
[Your Address]
[Your Contact Details]
Date: [Date]

Subject: Complaint against Legal Practitioners and Their Firms for Facilitating the Unlawful Deprivation of Parental Rights

Dear Sir/Madam,

I, [Your Full Name], wish to lodge a formal complaint against the following legal practitioners and their respective firms:

1. [Legal Practitioner 1 Full Name], [Firm Name]
2. [Legal Practitioner 2 Full Name], [Firm Name]
3. [Add more if applicable]

I am the biological father of [Child's Full Name], born on [Date of Birth]. The child's biological mother is [Mother's Full Name].

On [Date], the mother unlawfully and intentionally deprived me of my parental rights and responsibilities over our child by [Describe the actions taken by the mother, e.g., unilaterally relocating with the child without consent, denying access to the child, etc.]. I believe that the above-mentioned legal practitioners and their firms have facilitated or endorsed this unlawful deprivation of my parental rights by [Describe the actions taken by legal practitioners and their firms, e.g., pursuing settlements or issuing court orders that unfairly discriminate against the father].

I assert that these actions by the legal practitioners and their firms are in violation of the equality provisions enshrined in the Constitution of the Republic of South Africa, 1996, the Children's Act 38 of 2005, and the Promotion of Equality and Prevention of Unfair Discrimination Act 4 of 2000 (PEPUDA). Section 9 of the Constitution guarantees equality before the law and prohibits unfair discrimination on various grounds, including gender. The Children's Act and PEPUDA further reinforce these principles.

The Constitutional Court, in President of the Republic of South Africa v Hugo 1997 (4) SA 1 (CC), affirmed that there is no rule of law that favours mothers over fathers or vice versa. Equality before the law means that both parents have equal rights and responsibilities from the moment of the child's conception. This right is effective from the day the Constitution came into effect and applies equally to both parents from the day they assert their rights.

Furthermore, in the recent case of Van Wyk and Others v Minister of Employment and Labour [2023] ZAGPPHC 1213, the High Court emphasised the importance of parental equality and the need to eliminate unfair discrimination between mothers and fathers in the context of parental leave.

I contend that these actions by the legal practitioners and their firms are in breach of their ethical duties under the Code of Conduct for All Legal Practitioners, Candidate Legal Practitioners and Juristic Entities (the Code). Specifically, I believe that they have violated:

1. **Rule 3.3**, which requires legal practitioners to act in the best interests of their clients, subject to their duty to the court, the interests of justice, the observance of the law, and the maintenance of ethical standards;
2. **Rule 3.5**, which prohibits legal practitioners from doing anything that may place them in a position where their own interests conflict with those of their clients or the interests of justice;
3. **Rule 3.15**, which requires legal practitioners to refrain from doing anything that could bring the legal profession into disrepute; and
4. **Rule 59.2**, which mandates legal practitioners to take active steps to ensure that any settlement in a matter involving the care and residence of children is equitable to all parties and in the best interests of the children.

These actions are not only in breach of the Code of Conduct but also in contravention of the equality provisions in the Constitution of the Republic of South Africa, 1996, the Children's Act 38 of 2005, and the Promotion of Equality and Prevention of Unfair Discrimination Act 4 of 2000 (PEPUDA). Their actions may subject them to sanctions, both criminal and otherwise, under these laws.

Moreover, the burden of proof lies with the party claiming that a father should not have equal parental rights and responsibilities, not on the father asserting his rights. Any party interfering with a father's assertion of equal rights without providing constitutionally valid reasons is in breach of the highest law of the land.

In support of my complaint, I attach the following evidence:

1. [List and attach relevant documents, such as court orders, correspondence, etc.]
2. [List and attach any other relevant evidence, such as witness statements, recordings, etc.]

I request that the Legal Practice Council investigate this matter thoroughly and take appropriate disciplinary action against the legal practitioners and their firms involved, in accordance with the Legal Practice Act 28 of 2014 and the Code. Their conduct has caused me and my child undue hardship and distress, brought the legal profession into disrepute, and undermined the public's trust in the administration of justice.

I am willing to cooperate fully with the investigation and provide any further information or evidence as required. Thank you for your attention to this matter.

Sincerely,
[Your Signature]
[Your Full Name]

Criminal Complaint Affidavit to the National Prosecuting Authority of South Africa (NPA)

I, [Full Name], [ID Number], residing at [Address], do hereby make oath and state as follows:

1. I am the complainant in this matter, and unless otherwise stated, the facts contained herein are within my personal knowledge and are both true and correct.
2. I am the biological father of [Child's Full Name], born on [Date of Birth]. The child's biological mother is [Mother's Full Name].
3. On [Date], the mother unlawfully and intentionally deprived me of my parental rights and responsibilities over our child by [Describe the actions taken by the mother, e.g., unilaterally relocating with the child without consent, denying access to the child, etc.]. This deprivation is in violation of the equality provisions enshrined in the Constitution of the Republic of South Africa, 1996, the Children's Act 38 of 2005, and the Promotion of Equality and Prevention of Unfair Discrimination Act 4 of 2000 (PEPUDA).
4. Section 9 of the Constitution guarantees equality before the law and prohibits unfair discrimination on various grounds, including gender. The Children's Act and PEPUDA further reinforce these principles. The Constitutional Court, in President of the Republic of South Africa v Hugo 1997 (4) SA 1 (CC), affirmed that there is no rule of law that favours mothers over fathers or vice versa.
5. Equality before the law means that both parents have equal rights and responsibilities from the moment of the child's conception. This right is effective from the day the Constitution came into effect and applies equally to both parents from the day they assert their rights.
6. I have not consented to this deprivation of my parental rights and responsibilities, and I believe that the mother's actions constitute parental child abduction or kidnapping as defined in South African criminal law.
7. Furthermore, I believe that certain legal practitioners and courts have facilitated or endorsed this unlawful deprivation of my parental rights by [Describe the actions taken by legal practitioners and courts, e.g., pursuing settlements or issuing court orders that unfairly discriminate against the father]. These actions are not only unethical and unconstitutional but may also amount to accomplice liability for parental child abduction or kidnapping.
8. The recent High Court case of Van Wyk and Others v Minister of Employment and Labour [2023] ZAGPPHC 1213 emphasised the importance of parental equality and the need to eliminate unfair discrimination between mothers and fathers in the context of parental leave. This judgement further supports my contention that the deprivation of my parental rights is unlawful and discriminatory.
9. The burden of proof lies with the party claiming that a father should not have equal parental rights and responsibilities, not on the father asserting his rights. Any party interfering with a father's assertion of equal rights without providing constitutionally valid reasons is in breach of the highest law of the land.
10. In support of my complaint, I attach the following evidence: a) [List and attach relevant documents, such as court orders, correspondence, etc.] b) [List and attach any other relevant evidence, such as witness statements, recordings, etc.]
11. I request that the South African Police Service (SAPS) investigate this matter and take appropriate action against the alleged perpetrators, including the mother, legal practitioners, and courts involved, for their role in the unlawful deprivation of my parental rights and responsibilities.
12. I am willing to cooperate fully with the investigation and provide any further information or evidence as required.

THUS SIGNED AND SWORN before me at [Place] on this [Day] day of [Month], [Year], the deponent having acknowledged that he/she knows and understands the contents of this affidavit, has no objection to taking the prescribed oath, and considers the oath to be binding on his/her conscience.

COMMISSIONER OF OATHS
Full name:
Designation:
Area:

Commission for Gender Equality (CGE)

To: The Commission for Gender Equality
[CGE Address]
From: [Your Full Name]
[Your Address]
[Your Contact Details]
Date: [Date]

Subject: Complaint of Gender Discrimination – Case No. [Case Number]
Dear Sir/Madam,
I am lodging a formal complaint of gender discrimination against [Children's Court/Magistrate's Name], in relation to [Case Number].

- **Nature of Complaint:** [Describe the specific instances of gender discrimination you experienced, referencing the maternal preference rule and any biassed statements or actions by court officials].

- **Impact:** Explain how this discrimination has negatively affected you and your child.

- **Evidence:** Attach evidence supporting your claim of gender discrimination.

- **Relief Sought:** Request a: thorough investigation into the discriminatory practices of the Children's Court, Recommendations for policy and procedural changes to eliminate gender bias in child custody cases, Training and education for judicial officers on gender equality and the best interests of the child, a review of your case to ensure a fair and unbiased determination based on the child's best interests.

I believe the actions of the Children's Court violate the constitutional right to equality and the principle of the best interests of the child.
Thank you for your attention to this matter.

Sincerely,
Full Names & signature

The Public Protector

[Your Full Name]

    [Your Address]

    [Your Contact Details]

    [Date]

    The Public Protector

    [Address of the Public Protector's Office]

    Dear Public Protector,

    Subject: Complaint Regarding Discrimination Against Fathers in Children's Courts and the High Court's Failure to Uphold Its Duties as Upper Guardian

    I, [Your Full Name], hereby lodge a formal complaint concerning the systemic discrimination against fathers in children's court proceedings and the High Court's failure to address this issue in its capacity as the upper guardian of all children.

Background and History of the Complaint:

The children's courts in South Africa have consistently applied the maternal preference rule, which unfairly favours mothers in custody and parental rights cases. This practice is not only contrary to the equality provision in the Constitution but also undermines the best interests of the child. Fathers are subjected to additional requirements and burdens, such as the payment of damages, the need to approach a court to access their equal rights, and the imposition of evaluations by the family advocate, which are not applicable to mothers. This state-sanctioned discrimination persists despite the absence of such discrimination against women in formal education and the workplace, where affirmative action measures are in place to integrate them.

Reasons for Requesting an Investigation by the Public Protector:

The High Court, as the upper guardian, has failed to fulfil its duties by allowing this injustice to continue unabated. The discrimination against fathers in children's courts robs children of the full involvement of both parents, which is crucial for their well-being and development. The persistence of this discrimination in 2024, despite the constitutional provisions and the evolving societal norms, is a reflection of the High Court's failure to exercise its oversight powers effectively. This failure has contributed to the challenges faced by the children born after the constitution, who now languish as adults in a country plagued by high youth unemployment, excessive levels of violence and crime, gender-based violence, and failing education and state institutions.

Steps Taken to Resolve the Issue:

[Describe any efforts you have made to address this issue, such as engaging with the children's courts, the High Court, or other relevant authorities. Provide details of any correspondence, complaints, or legal actions taken, and the outcomes of these efforts.]

Supporting Documents:

[List and attach any relevant documents, such as court orders, affidavits, research papers, or other evidence that supports your complaint and highlights the discrimination against fathers and the High Court's failure to address the issue.]

Preferred Outcome:

I request that the Public Protector investigate the systemic discrimination against fathers in children's courts and the High Court's failure to uphold its duties as the upper guardian. I hope that this investigation will lead to recommendations for legal and institutional reforms to ensure that fathers are treated equally in parental rights matters and that the best interests of the child are truly prioritised. I also request that the Public Protector examine instances where mothers have withheld children from fathers, amounting to kidnapping, and the role of the High Court in addressing such cases.

I declare that the information provided in this complaint is true and accurate to the best of my knowledge. I am willing to cooperate fully with any investigation conducted by the Public Protector and provide further information or evidence as required.

Thank you for your attention to this matter.

Sincerely,

[Your Signature]

[Your Full Name]

The South African Law Reform Commission (SALRC)

[Your Full Name]
[Your Address]
[Your Contact Details]
[Date]

The Secretary

South African Law Reform Commission
[Address of the SALRC]

Dear Secretary,

Subject: Request for Investigation into Discrimination Against Fathers in Children's Courts and the Need for Legal Reform

I, [Your Full Name], hereby request that the South African Law Reform Commission (SALRC) conduct an investigation into the discrimination against fathers in children's court proceedings and the need for legal reform to ensure gender equality and the best interests of the child.

1. Background and Motivation

The children's courts in South Africa have consistently applied the maternal preference rule, which unfairly favours mothers in custody and parental rights cases. This practice is contrary to the equality provision in the Constitution and undermines the best interests of the child. The Children's Act explicitly discriminates against fathers by imposing additional requirements, such as the payment of damages, the need to approach a court to access their equal rights, and the imposition of evaluations by the family advocate, which are not applicable to mothers.

This state-sanctioned discrimination has persisted despite the absence of such discrimination against women in formal education and the workplace, where affirmative action measures are in place to integrate them. The consequences of this discrimination are evident in the challenges faced by children born after the constitution, who now languish as adults in a country plagued by high youth unemployment, excessive levels of violence and crime, gender-based violence, and failing education and state institutions.

2. Alignment with SALRC Selection Criteria

The investigation into the discrimination against fathers in children's courts aligns with the SALRC's selection criteria, as it is a predominantly legal issue that requires law reform to address the inconsistencies and unconstitutionality of the current practices. The potential benefits to society are significant, as addressing this discrimination would promote gender equality, ensure the best interests of the child, and contribute to the development of a more just and equitable legal system. The investigation would also advance the SALRC's mandate of promoting the development, improvement, modernization, and reform of the law in South Africa.

3. Proposed Scope and Methodology:

The investigation should examine the legal framework governing parental rights and responsibilities, including the Children's Act, and identify the provisions that discriminate against fathers. The investigation should also analyse the practices and decisions of children's courts, the role of the High Court as the upper guardian, and the impact of the maternal preference rule on the rights of fathers and the well-being of children. The methodology could include legal research, public consultations, expert input from family law specialists and child psychologists, and a comparative analysis of international best practices in parental rights and gender equality.

4. Potential Impact and Outcomes:

The investigation could lead to recommendations for amendments to the Children's Act and other relevant legislation to eliminate the discriminatory provisions and ensure equal treatment of fathers in parental rights matters. It could also result in guidelines for children's courts and the High Court to prioritise the best interests of the child and avoid the application of the maternal preference rule. The reforms resulting from the investigation would contribute to the realisation of gender equality, promote the active involvement of both parents in their children's lives, and create a legal system that truly upholds the rights and well-being of children.

5. Supporting Documents:

[List and attach any relevant documents, such as research papers, case law, international conventions, or other evidence that supports your request for an investigation and highlights the need for legal reform in this area.]

I believe that an investigation by the SALRC into the discrimination against fathers in children's courts is both necessary and timely. I am committed to assisting the SALRC in any way possible, and I am willing to provide further information or input as required.

Thank you for considering this request.

Sincerely,

[Your Signature]

[Your Full Name]

The Equality Court

FORM 2 Guide

INSTITUTION OF PROCEEDINGS IN TERMS OF SECTION 20 OF THE PROMOTION OF EQUALITY AND PREVENTION OF UNFAIR DISCRIMINATION ACT (ACT NO. 4 OF 2000)

PART A: PARTICULARS OF COMPLAINANT

Surname: [Your Surname]

Full names: [Your Full Names]

ID. No./Date of birth: [Your ID Number/Date of Birth]

Residential address: [Your Residential Address]

Residential telephone number: [Your Residential Telephone Number]

Cellular telephone number: [Your Cellular Telephone Number]

Work address: [Your Work Address]

Work telephone number: [Your Work Telephone Number]

Fax number: [Your Fax Number]

Physical address (where documents can be served): [Your Physical Address]

Preferred method in which the form is to be served: [Choose one: Registered post, E-mail, Fax, Sheriff, Clerk]

Correspondence contact details: [Your Correspondence Contact Details]

E-mail address: [Your Email Address]

PART B: PARTICULARS OF PERSON ACTING IN TERMS OF SECTION 20(1)(b) - (f) ON BEHALF OF ANOTHER PERSON/ASSOCIATION/BODY

[Leave this section blank if you are acting on your own behalf]

PART C: PARTICULARS OF RESPONDENT(S)

Name of person(s)/organisation(s) against whom/which proceedings are instituted:

1. [Mother's Full Name], ID No./Date of birth: [Mother's ID Number/Date of Birth]

2. [Legal Representative 1 Full Name], ID No./Date of birth: [Legal Representative 1 ID Number/Date of Birth], [Law Firm Name]

3. [Legal Representative 2 Full Name], ID No./Date of birth: [Legal Representative 2 ID Number/Date of Birth], [Law Firm Name]

4. Children's Court for the District of [District Name]

5. High Court of South Africa, [Division Name]

[Provide the relevant contact details, addresses, and preferred method of service for each respondent]

PART D: PARTICULARS OF PERSON APPEARING ON BEHALF OF COMPLAINANT

[Provide the details of your legal representative, if applicable]

PART E: PARTICULARS OF COMPLAINT AND RELIEF SOUGHT

Nature of complaint:

The complaint relates to the systemic discrimination against fathers in the allocation of parental rights and responsibilities by the Children's Court, facilitated by the mother and her legal representatives, and the failure of the High Court to address this issue as the upper guardian of all minor children. The specific incidents of discrimination include:

1. The application of the maternal preference rule by the Children's Court, which unfairly favours mothers in custody and parental rights cases, violating the equality clause in the Constitution and the best interests of the child principle.

2. The mother's actions in denying the father equal parental rights and responsibilities, and the legal representatives' facilitation of this unconstitutional stance.

3. The imposition of additional burdens on fathers seeking to enforce their parental rights, such as the payment of damages and the requirement to prove their suitability as parents, which are not applied to mothers.

4. The High Court's failure to exercise its oversight powers and address the systemic discrimination against fathers in the Children's Court, despite its role as the upper guardian of all minor children.

These discriminatory practices have resulted in the father being denied equal parental rights and responsibilities, and the child being deprived of the full involvement and care of both parents, which is detrimental to their best interests and well-being.

How has it affected you?

The discrimination against fathers in the Children's Court has caused immense emotional distress, financial strain, and damage to the father-child relationship. The father has been unjustly deprived of his constitutional right to equality and the opportunity to be an active and equal participant in his child's life. The child has been denied the benefits of a nurturing relationship with their father, which is crucial for their emotional, psychological, and social development.

Documents:

[List and attach any relevant documents, such as court orders, affidavits, correspondence, or other evidence that supports your complaint]

Relief sought:

1. A declaratory order that the maternal preference rule and the discriminatory practices against fathers in the Children's Court are unconstitutional and invalid.

2. An order directing the Children's Court and the High Court to apply the law in a manner that upholds the equality clause and the best interests of the child principle, without unfair discrimination against fathers.

3. An order compelling the mother and her legal representatives to respect and facilitate the father's equal parental rights and responsibilities.

4. An order for the payment of damages by the respondents, jointly and severally, for the emotional distress, financial loss, and other harm suffered by the father and the child as a result of the discriminatory practices.

5. An order directing the respondents to issue a public apology acknowledging the discriminatory nature of their actions and committing to rectify their practices.

6. Any other relief that the court deems just and equitable.

PART F: PARTICULARS OF INSTITUTIONS/BODIES APPROACHED

Particulars of institutions/bodies previously approached in respect of the complaint:

1. Complaint to the Magistrates Commission regarding the conduct of magistrates in applying the maternal preference rule and discriminating against fathers.

2. Complaint to the Legal Practice Council against the mother's legal representatives for facilitating the discriminatory practices and breaching their ethical duties.

3. Complaint to the National Prosecuting Authority regarding the potential criminal liability of the mother and legal representatives for parental child abduction or kidnapping.

4. Submission to the South African Law Reform Commission requesting an investigation into the discriminatory practices in the Children's Court and the need for legal reform.

5. Complaint to the Public Protector regarding the unconstitutional and discriminatory practices in the Children's Court and the High Court's failure to address the issue.

The response of the institutions/bodies mentioned above:
[Provide a summary of the responses received from each institution/body, if any]

PART G: AFFIDAVIT

I, [Your Full Name], hereby make oath and say that:

1. I am an adult male residing at [Your Address]. I am the complainant in this matter, and the facts contained herein are within my personal knowledge and belief, unless otherwise stated or indicated by the context.

2. I am the biological father of [Child's Full Name], born on [Child's Date of Birth]. The child's biological mother is [Mother's Full Name].

3. Since the birth of my child, I have been subjected to systemic discrimination by the Children's Court in the allocation of parental rights and responsibilities. The court has consistently applied the maternal preference rule, which unfairly favors mothers in custody and parental rights cases, violating the equality clause in the Constitution and the best interests of the child principle.

4. The mother of my child, [Mother's Full Name], has actively denied me equal parental rights and responsibilities, and her legal representatives, [Legal Representative 1 Full Name] and [Legal Representative 2 Full Name], have facilitated this unconstitutional stance.

5. I have been subjected to additional burdens in seeking to enforce my parental rights, such as the payment of damages and the requirement to prove my suitability as a parent, which are not applied to mothers. This differential treatment is discriminatory and unjust.

6. Despite my efforts to assert my parental rights and challenge the discriminatory practices in the Children's Court, the High Court, as the upper guardian of all minor children, has failed to exercise its oversight powers and address the systemic discrimination against fathers.

7. The discriminatory practices have caused me immense emotional distress, financial strain, and damage to my relationship with my child. I have been unjustly deprived of my constitutional right to equality and the opportunity to be an active and equal participant in my child's life.

8. My child has been denied the benefits of a nurturing relationship with their father, which is crucial for their emotional, psychological, and social development. The discriminatory practices in the Children's Court are detrimental to the best interests and well-being of my child.

9. I have approached various institutions and bodies, including the Magistrates Commission, the Legal Practice Council, the National Prosecuting Authority, the South African Law Reform Commission, and the Public Protector, to address the discriminatory practices and seek redress. However, the responses received have been inadequate, and the systemic discrimination persists.

10. I have attached the following documents in support of my complaint:

a. [List and describe the relevant documents, such as court orders, correspondence, or other evidence]

b. [List and describe any additional supporting documents]

11. I am instituting these proceedings in the Equality Court as a last resort to challenge the unconstitutional and discriminatory practices in the Children's Court and to seek relief that upholds the principles of equality and the best interests of the child.

12. I pray that this Honourable Court grants the relief sought in my complaint, including declaratory orders, mandatory orders, damages, and any other relief that the court deems just and equitable.

____

DEPONENT

I certify that:

a. The Deponent acknowledged to me that:

i. He knows and understands the contents of this declaration;

ii. He has no objection to taking the prescribed oath; and

iii. He considers the prescribed oath as binding on his conscience.

b. The Deponent thereafter uttered the words "I swear that the contents of this declaration are true, so help me God."

c. The Deponent signed this declaration in my presence at ___________________ on this _______ day of ___________________ 20____.

____

COMMISSIONER OF OATHS
Full names:
Designation:
Area:
Address:

This affidavit template follows the structure and content of the complaint, providing a personal account of the father's experiences of discrimination in the Children's Court, the involvement of the mother and her legal representatives, and the High Court's failure to address the issue. The affidavit also highlights the emotional, financial, and relational impact of the discriminatory practices on the father and the child.

By signing the affidavit before a Commissioner of Oaths, the father attests to the truthfulness of the contents of the complaint and the supporting documents, lending credibility to the application to the Equality Court.

By approaching the Equality Court as the final step in the legal strategy, after engaging with other relevant institutions and bodies, the father aims to comprehensively challenge the systemic discrimination and seek relief that addresses the unconstitutional practices and upholds the principles of equality and the best interests of the child.

Afterword: An Open Letter to My Son

Dear Son,

As I write this, you are still a young child, blissfully unaware of the struggles and challenges that have shaped your early years. By the time you are old enough to read and understand these words, I hope that the world you, Solo, and your cousins inhabit will be a far more just and equitable place than the one in which I have fought my battles.

From the moment I first thought of you as nothing but a hope and guiding light in the future until I held you in my arms, I knew that I would move mountains to ensure your happiness, your safety, and your right to a future filled with love and opportunity. Long before you were born, just at the prospect of you, I shaped and worked towards a future that would be conducive for you. Little did I know then that this commitment would lead me down a path of legal battles, personal sacrifices, and a relentless fight against a system that seemed determined to deny me my rightful place in your life.

As a father, I have always believed that my role in your upbringing is equal to that of your mother. The love, guidance, and support that I have to offer you are no less valuable or essential than hers. And yet, at every turn, I have found myself confronted by a legal system and a society that sought to diminish my importance, to relegate me to the status of a secondary parent.

I could not accept this. I could not stand by and watch as outdated biases and discriminatory practices, such as the maternal preference rule and the unequal application of parental rights, threatened to rob you of the nurturing presence of your father. And so, I fought. I fought for my rights, for your rights, and for the rights of countless other fathers who found themselves in similar situations.

My battle has not been an easy one. As I detailed throughout this book, I have faced setbacks, frustrations, and moments of despair. I have navigated the complex labyrinth of the South African family law system, exposing the systemic discrimination against fathers in children's court proceedings. I have challenged the unconstitutional application of the maternal preference rule and advocated for the equal recognition of fathers' parental rights and responsibilities.

But through it all, I have drawn strength from the unconditional love I have for you and from the unwavering conviction that my fight is a just and necessary one. I have been inspired by the stories of other fathers who have joined me in this struggle, united in our determination to create a more equitable society for our children.

As you grow older and begin to navigate the complexities of this world, I want you to know that my fight has not just been about our family. It has been about creating a society where every child has the opportunity to benefit from the love, guidance, and support of both their parents, regardless of their gender or marital status.

I dream of a future where the principles of equality and the best interests of the child are not just lofty ideals enshrined in law books but living, breathing realities that shape the lives of every family. A future where fathers are no longer relegated to the sidelines but are recognized and valued as equal partners in the raising of their children.

I know that change does not happen overnight. The biases and inequities that I have fought against, as exposed in this book, are deeply entrenched in our legal system and societal norms. It will take the collective efforts of many to dismantle them. But I also know that every battle fought, every voice raised in protest, brings us one step closer to the world I envision for you.

My son, as you embark on your own journey through life, I hope that the lessons of my struggle, chronicled in these pages, will serve as a source of inspiration and guidance. I hope that you will never accept injustice or inequality as inevitable but will always have the courage to stand up for what is right, even in the face of adversity.

And above all, I want you to always know the depth of my love for you. Every sacrifice I have made, every battle I have fought in this war against discrimination, has been for you and for the countless other children, like Solo and your cousins, who deserve to grow up in a world where they are cherished, nurtured, and valued by both their parents. State-sanctioned discrimination is not in your best interest as a child, and I will continue to fight until true equality is achieved.

With all my love,
Your Father